The Human
Revolution

Series edited by Paul Johnstone *and* Anna Ritchie

Author and publishers join together in commending this book to the memory of the late Paul Johnstone

The Human Revolution

from Ape to Artist

Desmond
Collins

PHAIDON·OXFORD
E. P. DUTTON·NEW YORK

I would like to thank all those people who have helped me in any way with the production of this book and all those whose work I have drawn upon. I would especially like to thank Sally Kington who contributed so much to the text in its final form.

I dedicate this book to my wife Ann.

Phaidon Press Limited, Littlegate House, St Ebbe's Street, Oxford
Published in the United States of America by E. P. Dutton & Co., Inc.

First published 1976

© 1976 Desmond Collins

ISBN: hardback   0 7148 1676 0
       paperback 0 7148 1721 X
Library of Congress Catalog Card Number: 76-5359

Filmset in Great Britain by BAS Printers Limited, Wallop, Hampshire

Printed in Italy by Amilcare Pizzi SpA, Milan

Contents

	Introduction	7
Chapter I	The Discovery of Early Man	8
Chapter II	The Great Ice Ages	31
Chapter III	Apes and Human Ancestry	63
Chapter IV	The First Men	83
Chapter V	Neanderthal Man	111
Chapter VI	The Cave Artists	130
Chapter VII	Hunting Societies	160
Chapter VIII	The Rise and Fall of Cromagnon Man	187
	List of illustrations	199
	Index	204

Introduction

This book charts the course of two revolutions and describes the events leading up to a third.

It chronicles first of all a revolution in thought when, only just over a hundred years ago, it became impossible to deny overwhelming evidence presented by the Darwinians for man's animal ancestry.

It was then that the full story of man's break with the animal world began to come to light. A slow physical and cultural evolution became apparent. Mastery of stone tool-making and a new-found success as a hunter, the emergence of family life and the development of speech were seen to have constituted our second revolution, the original Human Revolution.

Our third revolution was the result of two million years of increasing technical proficiency culminating in a host of fundamental inventions, including the bow and arrow, and in the brilliance of the painted caves of Lascaux and Altamira. Domestication of plants and animals led to a controlled food supply and the beginning of a settled life, bringing an end to the nomadic ways of ice age man.

Facing page *Black paintings on the walls of the 'shaft of the dead man' at Lascaux. The first absolute date for ice age hunters came from this part of the cave.*

Chapter I   The Discovery
of Early Man

In 1950, and only four years after he had originally conceived the technique of radiocarbon dating, Nobel prize-winning physicist Willard F. Libby announced his first result from dating the Old Stone Age. He estimated 15,516 years as the age of a piece of silver fir charcoal found deep inside the world famous painted cave of Lascaux. Painted caves were the work of Cromagnon man and belong to the latest division of the Old Stone Age, technically called the Upper Palaeolithic period. The figure is mind-boggling, but, far from considering it too old, most specialists had expected a higher figure. As a matter of fact, later estimates for the occupation of Lascaux are a little higher, but the important point is that geologists and archaeologists routinely think in terms of hundreds of thousands or millions of years.

How did it come about that by Libby's time scientists interested in our remote antiquity took it for granted that man had existed much more than ten thousand years? Certainly only a hundred years before, such an estimate would have been quite unacceptable to most people who had any views on it. They would have believed that no men were older than Adam and that it was quite obvious from the Old Testament that Adam had lived only a few thousand years before Christ. 4004 BC was the favoured date for the creation of the world and Bishop Lightfoot felt able to specify that it was at 9 am on the 23rd of October in that year.

The answer is that, in the twenty years between 1850 and 1870, a profound change came over the outlook of the scientific world. Some of its fondest beliefs were shattered, most obviously by Darwin's *The Origin of Species*, but also by a whole series of parallel developments.

John Frere
In 1797 the squire of Roydon Hall, a few miles from Diss on the borders of Norfolk and Suffolk, wrote a letter to the secretary of the Society of

Antiquaries in London. The squire's name was John Frere; he described some observations he had made in the brick-clay pit at Hoxne, four miles south-east of Diss. The letter was published in 1800 in the journal *Archaeologia* and has since become famous as a landmark in the recognition of human antiquity.

Frere was already 57 years of age and a man of some standing. He had been High Sheriff of Suffolk and in the last years of his life he was MP for Norwich. His letter described and illustrated some fine pointed stone tools of a type which have since come to be called handaxes. They were, he suggested, 'fabricated and used by a people who had not yet the use of metals . . . The situation in which these weapons were found may tempt us to refer them to a very remote period indeed; even beyond that of the present world'.

Geology and catastrophes

The remark about Hoxne being inhabited in a remote period, 'beyond that of the present world', is a reminder of the dominant philosophy in geology at this time. A lot had been learned about the rock strata which made up the earth's crust and a systematic study of the enigmatic 'fossils' they contained was just beginning. But how the strata had formed and why they contained fossils was disputed.

Until about 1830 the prevailing view of geology was 'catastrophism', advocated in its most developed form by Baron Georges Cuvier, the 'Pope of Bones' and later French Minister of the Interior designate, and by his English associate Dean William Buckland. This view maintained that the strata of the earth were the result of successive catastrophes or deluges. Like Noah's flood, they had wiped out all the unsuspecting animals, who had become entombed in the strata as fossils. In the absence of an ark, new arrivals had to be created after each catastrophe. Man could not possibly be contemporary with extinct animals, for we know from Genesis that he was created along with all the animals of the 'present world'. Catastrophism had no room for Frere's evidence of men fabricating stone tools in the remote past.

Two men were particularly associated with the downfall of catastrophist geology. They were James Hutton of Edinburgh and Charles Lyell, also a Scot, living in London. Hutton died in 1797, the year of Frere's letter, having proposed and argued the principle that geological strata could best be explained by the operation of known forces, such as the laying down of deposits observable today, operating over an immensely long time.

Lyell, born coincidentally in 1797, brought these ideas to fruition. His influential three volume treatise of 1830–3, *Principles of Geology*, was subtitled 'Being an attempt to explain the former changes of the Earth's surface by reference to causes now in action'. This promoted Hutton's principles with great cogency and detail and is often regarded as the foundation stone of modern geology. It is not surprising that Frere made no reference to Hutton's ideas, even though he was a Fellow of the Royal Society, for Hutton's views were little known before the nineteenth century, even in Britain.

There is a key sentence in Hutton's explanation of geological strata: 'No powers are to be employed that are not natural to the globe, no action to be admitted except those of which we know the principle'. This preference for trying to understand the past in terms of the present is conveniently termed actualism (though Lyell used the more cumbersome term uniformitarianism).

The fundamentally different philosophy of catastrophism, on the other hand, regularly invoked upheavals which have no modern parallel. Some kind of intervention by a higher power was often assumed to account for such phenomena as the appearance of new species. Catastrophists thought that new animal types came 'from elsewhere', there being no apparent desire to find a natural explanation. This kind of 'over there' philosophy has a counterpart in the field of biological and human history.

Hutton believed that, on the whole, strata accumulated gradually. Accordingly the great thicknesses of some strata implied immense periods of time; Hutton's followers were the first to insist on this enormous length of geological time and the millions of years in which it must be measured.

Evolution by natural selection

According to catastrophist biology, man, like other animals, was the result of a sudden act of creation; once created he had not changed physically, for species are immutable. Nor had he advanced much mentally or culturally. In fact he had probably degenerated. Man could not be an animal—a thought abhorrent to the Victorians—and no intermediate types between him and animals could ever have existed.

The biological counterpart of actualism is evolution which contradicted almost completely the position of the catastrophists. Gradual evolution replaced sudden creation; it presupposed that species could change greatly over time and it made possible the belief in a common ancestor for currently diverse species including man, who took his place among the animals.

From the point of view of the archaeologist, it made sense of the discovery of stone tools and the like in deposits of great age. They could now contribute to our species history, and it became obvious that man was the contemporary both of the extinct animals and of the ice age.

There is little doubt that Charles Darwin was the key figure in making evolution acceptable. People before him, including his grandfather Erasmus, had suggested that animal species might undergo transformation.

10

Charles Darwin, founder of modern evolutionary theory.

Sir Charles Lyell, founder of modern geology.

Sir John Evans, leading archaeologist in the Darwinian circle.

Handaxe obtained by John Evans during his visit to Amiens in 1859 when the true antiquity of man was confirmed.

He had noted in the 1830s that a population of animals always exhibits considerable variation and that this sometimes includes 'varieties', like the island finches of the Galapagos, that were well on their way to becoming separate species. What was still lacking was an adequate mechanism to explain the consistent change needed for new species to emerge and an adequate theory to explain how new features could appear.

As Darwin and Wallace realized independently, the mechanism was available amongst speculations in Thomas Malthus' *Essay on Population*. He spoke of the inevitable 'struggle for survival' among populations. The fact that not all survive this struggle is the basis of natural selection. Natural animal populations have more offspring than survive; the reasonable deduction from this is that, out of the range of characters present in the population, those which help their owner to survive will be more often passed on to later generations.

How the characters are passed on, and how new ones arise, came to be understood only slowly and imperfectly at the beginning of the twentieth century. This, in spite of the fact that Gregor Mendel's unpublicized researches had already gone a long way to solving this problem with his laws of heredity.

Kent's Cavern and the Somme

Two early archaeological investigations culminating in the late 1850s made a decisive contribution to the Darwinian revolution. Kent's Cavern is a big cave in the Devonian limestone near Torquay. Successive amateurs had tried digging in the deposits which make up the floor of the cave and had found extinct animals in abundance, even the long extinct sabre-toothed tiger. Persistent reports came back of stone tools from the same levels. 'Impossible', said Dean Buckland, true to the catastrophist position, 'the deposits must be mixed'.

Finally, in 1858, a committee of the prestigious British Association for the Advancement of Science was appointed to look into the question. An energetic local naturalist, William Pengelly, directed the digging, and it was decided to continue in Kent's Cavern but also to try an undisturbed cave, the Windmill Hill cave, on the other side of Torbay. The results, triumphantly reported back to the Association, left no room for doubt that man had lived at the same time as the extinct animals.

The second exploration was in the Somme valley in northern France. Here a colourful local figure, Jaques Boucher de Perthes, had for years been visiting the gravel pits around Abbeville and collecting shaped stones he called 'haches' or axes. A poet in his youth, de Perthes held the position of chief of customs at Abbeville but devoted much time to antiquarian collecting. The axes were, he thought, the work of 'antediluvian man', for he was a great believer in the flood and similar cataclysms. Undoubtedly some of his finds were natural, and the jaw he found in 1863 turned out to be a fake; but most of his finds were genuine Stone Age tools. Because the 'axes' have no convenient name, it was suggested at one time that they should be called 'bouchers', after Boucher de Perthes, but this name never caught on.

In 1858 after years of neglect by French experts, Hugh Falconer, the greatest authority of the time on fossil bones, happened to be in Abbeville and heard of de Perthes' finds. He took a look and was immediately convinced that the matter merited further investigation. The following year a noted geologist Joseph Prestwich and the antiquarian John Evans visited the Somme to follow up Falconer's observations.

Evans has left us a graphic description of the events of May the 2nd, 1859: '. . . soon after seven the next morning M. Boucher de Perthes, the first discoverer of the stone axes we were in pursuit of, came to take us to some of the gravel pits from whence his collection had been derived . . . We then adjourned to the house of M. de Perthes which is a complete Museum from top to bottom, full of painting, old carvings, pottery etc. and with a wonderful collection of flint axes and implements found among the beds of gravel and evidently deposited at the same time with them—in fact the remains of a race of men who existed at the same time when the deluge or whatever was the origin of these gravel beds took place. One of the most remarkable features of the case is that nearly all if not quite all of the animals whose bones are found in the same beds as the axes are extinct. There is the mammoth, the rhinoceros, the Urus—a tiger etc. After the examination of his Museum M. de Perthes gave us a most sumptuous déjeuner à la fourchette and we then set off for Amiens . . . We proceeded to the pit where sure enough the edge of an axe was visible in an entirely undisturbed bed of gravel and eleven feet from the surface. We had a photographer with us to take a view of it so as to corroborate our testimony and had only time to get that done and collect some twelve or fifteen axes from the workmen in the Pit when we were forced to take the train again to Abbeville'.

The reports which Prestwich and Evans gave to the Royal Society and the Society of Antiquaries played a major part in satisfying doubts on the antiquity of man.

The bone caves of the Dordogne region
There can have been no setting for pioneer research into the antiquity of man more fascinating than the limestone gorges of the Dordogne in south-west France. And the caves and rock shelters found in a short stretch of the Vézère valley between Lascaux and the picturesque village of Les Eyzies eighteen kilometres downstream have dominated this work. Les Eyzies has been described as the capital of prehistory and not without some justification.

It was in 1863 that investigation began here, only a year or two after

The old château in the centre of Les Eyzies as Lartet and Christy saw it at the time of their pioneer excavations in the vicinity in the mid-nineteenth century. The building now houses the National Museum of this 'Capital of Prehistory'.

14

the antiquity of man was first seriously considered and before the broad divisions of prehistory had been fully mapped out. For five busy months a Frenchman and an Englishman, Edouard Lartet and Henry Christy organized the systematic digging of at least six caves. Workmen were employed and supervision was sporadic; in any case the art of distinguishing thin levels in the cave earth had not yet been developed, and the deposits were usually regarded as a unity. But in spite of this, the standard was hardly surpassed until the next century.

Lartet had been interested in fossil bones for years and had found two primitive ape fossils (called *Pliopithecus* and *Dryopithecus*) in Miocene deposits of ten to twenty million years ago in his native Gers region near the Pyrenees before 1850. A magistrate by profession, he had devoted more and more time to the study of fossils and to archaeology, and latterly, with Christy's financial help, he was able to work fully on these interests. At first his belief in the antiquity of man was not popular with the establishment and he was only belatedly recognized with a professorship at the Muséum d'Histoire Naturelle so near his death in 1871 that he never gave his first lecture.

Henry Christy was a wealthy London banker and industrialist who, from 1850 onwards, travelled around the world for reasons of health and acquired a unique collection of ethnographic material. Ethnography, the study of primitive peoples and their culture, was only just beginning and on his travels Christy met and inspired Edward Tylor to become the first professional anthropologist in Britain. For this reason he has been called the godfather of anthropology, the whole science of man. He came to prehistory only a few years before his death in 1865, but threw himself into it with such enthusiasm that the scale of his Dordogne project was not matched until recently, and his writings contain some fundamental insights.

The contact between Lartet and Christy was most fruitful. This is perhaps best indicated in their posthumous collected volume *Reliquiae Aquitanicae*, in which their important discoveries are beautifully and methodically illustrated. Christy describes the cave deposits in his own words: 'The deposits consist usually of accumulations of broken bones, various-sized pebbles of stone extraneous to the local formation and collected from the river-bed, nodules of flint from which flakes have been struck, innumerable fragments or chips detached in the first dressings of these cores, and countless thousands of blades of flint, varying in size from lance-heads long enough and stout enough to have been used against the largest animal, down to lancets no larger than the blade of a penknife, and piercing-instruments of the size of the smallest bodkin. These remains are usually intermixed with charcoal in dust and in small fragments, and extend to a depth in some cases of eight to ten feet, and a length of sixty to seventy feet.

'Besides these have been found a multitude of implements formed of bone or deer-horn, and equally proved to have been made there, by the presence of the remnants of the bones and horns from which they had been sawn, and by the implements themselves being often in an unfinished state. They consist of square chisel-shaped implements; round sharp-pointed awl-like tools, some of which may also have served as the spikes of fish-hooks; harpoon-shaped lance-heads, plain or barbed; arrow-heads, with many and sometimes double barbs, cut with wonderful vigour; and lastly eyed needles of compact bone, finely pointed, polished and drilled, with round eyes so small and regular that some of the most assured and acute believers in all other findings might well doubt whether indeed they could have been drilled with stone, until their actual repetition by the the very stone implements found with them has dispelled their honest doubts. More than this, all but two of the many deposits explored have given more or less of examples of ornamented work; and three of them (Les Eyzies, Laugerie Basse, and La Madelaine) drawings and sculptures of various animals, perfectly recognizable as such.'

One discovery illustrates particularly vividly how these researches finally settled the question whether man had been the contemporary of extinct animals like the mammoth. For there was always the possibility that the stone tools were with the reindeer and mammoth bones owing to some mysterious process of mixing. Edouard Lartet gives the following account: 'In May 1864 M. de Verneuil and our deceased friend Dr. Falconer having shown a desire to visit the caverns and other localities of the Dordogne which I had explored in company with my much regretted fellow-labourer the late Mr. H. Christy, I accompanied them in that excursion. We were at that time still excavating at the Madelaine, which had already furnished a number of those animal figures carved on bone or on reindeer antler, which were submitted last year to the inspection of the Academy.

'On our arrival the workmen had just discovered five broken pieces of a rather thin plate or slab of ivory, once forming part of a moderate-sized tusk of an Elephant. Having joined the pieces together, according to lines of junction marked out by the minute intricacies of fracture, I showed Dr. Falconer the numerous characteristic, though shallow, engraved lines, which seemed to me to indicate some animal forms. The practised eye of the celebrated palaeontologist, who has so well studied the Proboscidians, at once recognized the head of an Elephant; and he soon pointed out other parts of the body, and particularly, in the region of the neck, a bundle of descending lines, which recall the long shaggy hair characteristic of the Mammoth or Elephant of the Glacial Period. We know that this specific peculiarity, indicative of the sub-arctic habitat of an animal of this genus, had been verified, in 1799, by Mr. Adams of the Academy of Saint-Petersburg, by the remains of carcases of the same kind of Elephant (*Elephas primigenius*) imbedded, flesh and bone, in the ice near the mouth of the

R. Underwood, del. 1797.

Flint Weapon.

Red deer painted on the walls at Lascaux in the Vézère valley. There are more paintings here than in any other Palaeolithic cave, the main subjects being deer, horses and oxen.

Previous page Landmark in the recognition of the magnitude of human antiquity—one of the handaxes discovered in 1797 at Hoxne by John Frere.

Objects of flint and bone left by prehistoric man and found in the late Palaeolithic cave earths of the Dordogne region by Lartet and Christy. They published the drawings in their Reliquiae Aquitanicae *in 1875.*

Left *The Vézère valley looking downstream from Castelmerle. Les Eyzies is 15 kilometres further on and the intervening stretch of river passes some of the most important sites with evidence of ice age man in south-west France.*

Below *Block of consolidated cave earth, full of prehistoric occupational debris, found in a rock shelter at Les Eyzies.*

Lena. In the Geological Gallery of the Museum, a tuft of the long hair of the Mammoth can be seen'.

The woolly mammoth

The mammoth was the largest of the animals of the last ice age in Europe, and was similar in size to the Indian elephant, namely $2\frac{1}{2}$ to 3 metres high at the shoulder; an ancestral form of half a million years ago was five metres high at the shoulder.

The first mammoth bones to be recorded were found in 1577 at lake Lucerne; a Basle doctor thought they belonged to a giant, and the tusk was attributed to a unicorn. In 1663 Otto von Guericke, the Mayor of Magdeburg and a well-known scientific experimenter, reconstructed mammoth bones from Quedlinburg as a unicorn.

It was Nicolaus Witsen, the Dutch Ambassador to Moscow, who realized that mammoths were elephants, and it was he who reported back the fact well known to the Tungus and other Siberian natives that skeletons of a creature they called 'Mammut' were commonly found in Siberia. Indeed its tusks were widely traded in medieval times as ivory.

A fossil elephant was found in north London, near Grays Inn Lane, in 1690, with a stone 'handaxe' which still survives. This may have been a mammoth or more likely the species *Elephas antiquus*, the woodland

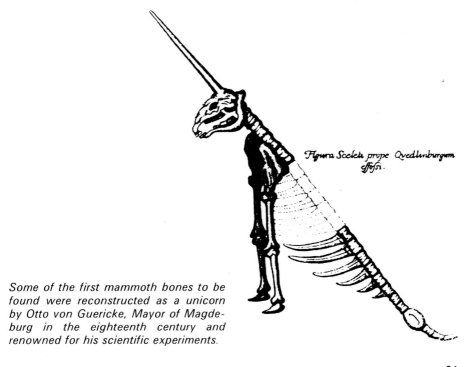

Some of the first mammoth bones to be found were reconstructed as a unicorn by Otto von Guericke, Mayor of Magdeburg in the eighteenth century and renowned for his scientific experiments.

elephant which was a contemporary of the mammoth. At the time it was ingeniously suggested that it was one of the elephants brought by the emperor Claudius in his invasion of Britain; and the handaxe belonged to an ancient Briton. In fact bones from various extinct species of elephant are among the commonest fossils from the ice age. Not only were the bones big and resistant to damage, but there probably was a genuine abundance of elephants.

The first case of a frozen mammoth carcase to be properly investigated was that found near the mouth of the Lena river in 1799. Professor Leith Adams was called in by the Russian authorities, and from his investigation it was first learnt that this type of elephant had a shaggy hairy coat. It seems to have been brownish-red in colour, although it may have changed colour somewhat in the tens of thousands of years since it was entombed. The hairy coat is obviously an adaptation to a colder climate than surviving elephants live in. We also know that a species of rhinoceros developed a hairy coat.

The Lena mammoth was known to Falconer, who realized that his recognition of an engraving of a mammoth on a piece of tusk in the Dordogne was conclusive evidence of the association of man and mammoth. In more recent years, of course, both the appearance of the mammoth and the style of ice age art could be copied by a well-informed forger, but in 1864 this was obviously out of the question. The conservative French scientific establishment, which until then had adhered to Cuvier's catastrophism, was now forced to accept the antiquity of man.

The frozen mammoth from the Lena was by no means the last such discovery. In 1901 a very well-preserved specimen was uncovered at Beresovska island in north-east Siberia and in 1949 a carcase was found on the Taimyr peninsula. How they came to be preserved is an intriguing question. Apparently favourable circumstances for this occur in the permanently frozen ground of northern Siberia, where, in the summer, streams cut channels in the fossil ice. In the winter these freeze over or fill with snow and silt. Heavy animals would break through the thin frozen crust and fall in. The winter cold is, and was in the ice ages, so extreme that prehistoric victims have sometimes remained frozen until the present day. The Beresovska mammoth was apparently trying to pull itself out of the freezing mud when it finally succumbed. Most of the frozen mammoths have dates of over 30,000 years according to the radiocarbon method, but the one from Taimyr is of a more recent date, about 9000 BC at the very close of the last ice age.

The discovery of frozen mammoths gives hope that one day a human body of similar remote antiquity may be found in a frozen state. For we have no idea what colour skin or sort of hair very early men had. His bones are sometimes found as fossils, for example on cave floors, but no amount of evidence of this kind can give us the details of his appearance.

The subdivisions of the Stone Age

One of the last of the Darwinian circle to become concerned with the problems of human antiquity was John Lubbock. His family were bankers and his father Sir J. W. Lubbock was an astronomer. They lived at High Elms in Orpington, close enough to the Darwin household at Down House to be frequent visitors. It is not surprising that Lubbock also visited fellow banker Henry Christy in the Dordogne in 1864.

Lubbock popularized the idea of three ages of prehistory, stone, bronze and iron, in common use among Scandinavian antiquaries since the 1840s. In 1868 he translated Professor Sven Nilsson's Swedish book of 1834, *Primitive Inhabitants of Scandinavia*, the first clear statement of the idea that men had been hunters in early times and that only later were pastoralism and agriculture introduced.

He emphasized the distinction between a New Stone Age with polished stone tools, for which archaeologists still use his term Neolithic, and an older Stone Age with only flaked stone tools, which he called Palaeolithic. The Palaeolithic, being earlier, was associated with extinct or migrated animals and no domestic forms. This absence of domestication has come to overshadow all other characteristics of the Palaeolithic.

Henry Christy's contribution to prehistory is easily overlooked since it is confined to the period of little over a year between his first writings on the subject in 1864 and his death a year later. More than anyone else he seems to have generalized the idea of a stone age in human history: '. . . we have broad ground for believing that the various races of men (though at widely different periods) have passed through what has been designated "the Age of Stone". These implements of stone are to be regarded as a grade of civilization, rather than any definite antiquity'. He also sketched out a subdivision of the Stone Age into a 'drift period' (the Somme gravels and Hoxne) which was earlier than a 'cave period' (le Moustier and la Madeleine for example) which in turn preceded a 'surface period'. Though much criticized, these ideas could be most fruitful, as we shall see.

Lubbock, Christy and Edward Tylor believed that the prehistoric past should be interpreted in terms of the present. Their view was that the way of life of surviving primitive peoples should be used as a guide to the understanding of our preliterate ancestors. This is the ethnographic approach to prehistory and is the third major application of actualism; this principle, as we have seen, was first used in Hutton's geology and was employed for a second time in Darwin's evolutionary biology. It has subsequently been argued that an ethnographic approach to prehistory can lead to serious errors.

The Darwinian achievement

The Darwinians and their contemporaries had made enormous strides in

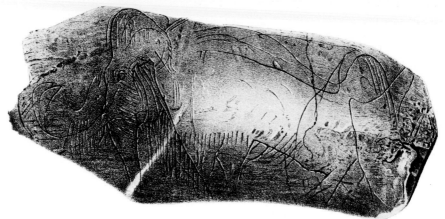

24

Above *One of the most famous of the 'deep-frozen' mammoths was found near Beresovska river in north-east Siberia. Dogs ate some of the flesh and a conference of scientists, assembled at Leningrad, were served soup made from its bones. It lived more than 39,000 years ago.*

Above left *In 1964 the skeletons of two elephants were found close together in a pit at Aveley in Essex. They belong to the time of the last interglacial. One is a mammoth, the other is the extinct woodland species* Elephas antiquus.

Below left *This piece of mammoth ivory, with a mammoth engraved on it, found in 1864 at la Madeleine, was the most dramatic possible demonstration that man had appeared before the mammoth became extinct.*

understanding man's origins. But dating early prehistoric sites, like Hoxne, in terms of years or even in terms of a small subdivision of geological time was a persistent problem. Lyell turned his attention to it briefly after 1859, and the result was a classic book, *The Geological Evidence of the Antiquity of Man*, published in 1863. He made the point that man had been, according to a multiplicity of indications, the contemporary of the extinct animals of the ice age. But how this could be made more specific and how much of the ice age was contemporary with early man, Lyell and his colleagues had no way of knowing. Indeed throughout the nineteenth century the main argument continued to be about whether there had been more than one ice age.

It was Edouard Lartet who took the only tentative steps towards solving this problem using the evidence of natural science. He considered the main fossil mammals in the sites and proposed the following scheme. The most recent period, with the wild ox—his Age of the Aurochs—could be regarded as the equivalent of what we now call the post-glacial period, after the disappearance of the reindeer from the middle latitudes. (Actually it is not at all clear how Lartet arrived at this division.) The Reindeer Age is a concept which was quite widely used, and because of the preponderance of reindeer at this time it is still a plausible way of describing the main last glacial cave occupation (from 10,000 BC back to 25,000 or even 60,000 BC). There is less validity in Lartet's earlier Mammoth and Cave Bear Age, though the cave bear is normally found to be earlier than 30,000 BC.

With continued use and modification, this scheme might have become a valuable tool. But it had some obvious shortcomings. The first is geographical: the reindeer may have left southern France at a particular time, but they may equally have survived further north, as they still do in Lapland. The scheme would only be worth using once circumscribed provinces of applicability had been drawn up. Secondly, it is quite common to find reindeer and wild ox together and the scheme would need to take this into account.

Darwin himself was reluctant to discuss the evolution of man, until finally he broke his silence in 1872 in *The Descent of Man*. The mechanism discussed for evolution in the animal world was clearly quite adequate for those who sought a natural origin for man. Thomas Henry Huxley, who so successfully defended Darwinism when it came under attack after the publication of *The Origin of Species*, made a systematic assessment of what was then known from comparison of man's anatomy and other physical characteristics with those of other animals. He concluded, as most modern authorities do, that African apes—the chimpanzee and the gorilla—are our closest relatives in the animal world. Darwin went on to draw the sensible conclusion that it was most likely that our ancestors originated in the same continent.

Huxley reviewed the scanty fossil evidence in *Man's Place in Nature*,

1863. A few 'Neanderthals' were known and some skeletons barely distinguishable from ourselves. Those skulls which differed from modern man differed in the direction of the apes, but Huxley argued that they were still quite close to man; they were not the elusive 'missing link' of popular journalism. Huxley had thirty years to wait for the discovery of Java man, the first really primitive fossil man to be recovered.

Lartet and Christy had found and published exquisite engraved and carved objects indicating a flourishing art style. But it was not until the end of the century, long after their deaths, that cave-wall art was first recognized. It was the excavation in 1896 of a cave called Pair-non-Pair, near Bordeaux, revealing engravings sealed under archaeological deposits, which provided some of the first hard evidence for the authenticity of cave-wall art. Font de Gaume and Les Combarelles, two caves explored near Les Eyzies in 1901, dispelled any remaining doubts.

By the 1870s the Darwinians were ceasing to be a major force in furthering the study of early man. The Darwinian achievement had been spectacular and is in no way diminished by the fact that their work was reaching an impasse. It was simply not clear where research into early man should next be directed. There was much to be done in the related fields of anatomy, physiology, geology and the archaeology of more recent periods. It was to these that they turned.

Evolution and diffusion

Of the pioneers in prehistory two men represent to a high degree the two extreme views of human culture. They are Gabriel de Mortillet, arch-evolutionist and major force in nineteenth century archaeology, and Sir Grafton Elliot Smith, arch-diffusionist, who, in the twentieth century, stood for the reaction against simple evolutionism. Evolutionism regards everything new as a development from what went before it. Diffusionism insists that anything new must have been imposed from elsewhere.

In the late 1860s de Mortillet proposed a solution to the dilemma of those who wanted, quite reasonably, to increase the precision of the dating of Palaeolithic sites. Geological methods such as the study of fauna were not helping much, so the archaeological evidence itself must be made the basis for dating. De Mortillet proceeded to create a series of archaeological epochs like those used in geology, but, instead of being defined by a series of fossils, they were defined by a series of archaeological types, and named from Palaeolithic sites in France; his names Mousterian, Solutrian and Magdalenian are still in use.

Underlying this scheme of epochs were two laws. His evolutionist law of progress stated that culture was improving continuously. He thought for example that the presence of bone tools indicated a higher stage of progress than the absence of bone tools and that we could fix the relative date of two sites by this principle. The order in which strata were laid down was deemed less important. His law of similar development stated that there is a single series of cultural stages through which all humanity passes. These stages were his archaeological epochs.

In the sense that he rejected catastrophism in any form, de Mortillet was ranged on the same side as the Darwinians. Later diffusionists were to return to the catastrophist practice of invoking unspecified outside sources for any new ideas or new people. But de Mortillet's way of looking at things did not allow this escape clause. If something new was seen to come in, then we had to try to understand its origin and not simply say: 'it was introduced from somewhere else'. Also, insofar as we still use his terms, we are admitting some validity to his divisions. Even today it is still often held as a broad generalization that Mousterian and Upper Palaeolithic (Solutrian and Magdalenian), as defined by de Mortillet from their archaeological characteristics, are equivalent to periods of time.

The shortcomings of de Mortillet's epochs are nevertheless so great that without modification they are simply misleading. The analogy with geological epochs founders on the fact that geological epochs are many millions of years long and their boundaries are believed to be valid no more precisely than to some thousands of years. Archaeological epochs, we now know, are often as little as a few thousand years long, and any time lag would destroy their usefulness as dating features.

Similarly, geologists usually use assemblages of fossils for dating in a relatively restricted area and expect to find different regional characteristics. We may say quite simply that extension of research into other continents in the twentieth century has shown that de Mortillet's later Palaeolithic epochs were quite local in character. An adequate theory of or even appreciation of geographical variation is lacking in de Mortillet's work.

Early in the twentieth century it was shown that preconceptions about the place of bone tools in progress were erroneous. Archaeologists argued, sometimes for good reasons and sometimes not, that the successive archaeological divisions (Magdalenian, Solutrian etc.) did not evolve into one another. S. H. Warren and Denis Peyrony held that distinctive assemblages of tools, each, to de Mortillet's mind, the hallmark of an epoch, were not even in all cases successive but were in use at one and the same time. In the 1920s V. Gordon Childe rationalized all this. In his view, prehistory had to be seen as an interaction of cultures and culture provinces, the archaeological equivalents of the tribes and territories of present-day primitive peoples. Each one would be subject to its own evolution. But this sane approach was overwhelmed by the rising tide of diffusionism. For diffusionists, local development played no part in culture change. As Lord Raglan put it: 'no savage ever invented anything'.

For Elliot Smith, Egypt was the fount of all progress; for others it was Mesopotamia or China, but it could have been almost anywhere. Elliot

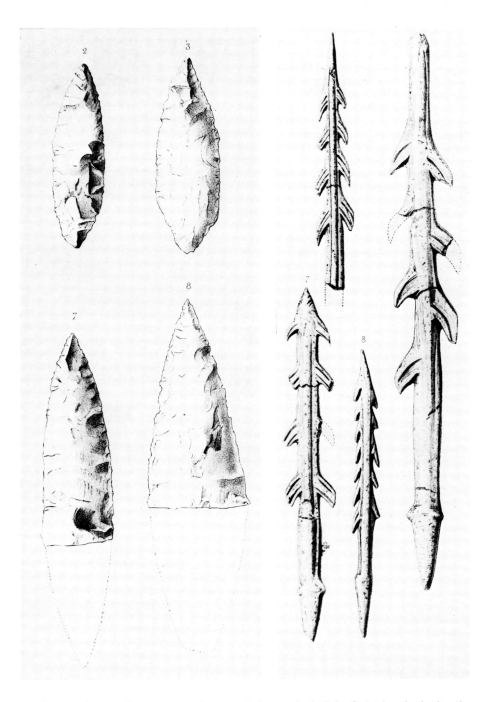

Leaf-shaped points have come to be regarded as typical of the Solutrian, barbed antler harpoons typical of the Magdalenian, the latest cave occupation of south-west France. De Mortillet made them the 'type fossils' of his Solutrian and Magdalenian epochs of the 'Upper', or later Palaeolithic.

Smith's followers believed that the 'Children of the Sun' had carried all higher or distinctive arts from Egypt to the corners of the globe: pyramids to central America; hieroglyphic writing to Peru; agriculture through the Mediterranean; circumcision and boomerangs to Australia. That modern authorities believe all these claims are false is largely beside the point. The point is that there was an overriding preconceived belief that this was the way of cultural advance and the evidence was not to be allowed to interfere with it.

So, in spite of de Mortillet's belief in the inevitability of progress, it is more than doubtful if Elliot Smith really did represent an advance on de Mortillet, or either of them on the Darwinians.

Despite continuing uncertainties, however, something of the huge antiquity of man had definitely been established. Now the precise nature of his relationship to the apes had to be determined, his ice age environment reconstructed and dated and the eventual amazing sophistication of his cave art brought to light.

Chapter II   **The Great Ice Ages**

Our place in geological time

The idea of millions of years is not easy to adjust to. Two million and two thousand million years both seem unimaginably long. The following analogy may help. If the history of the earth is a thousand page book, then the Alps came into existence three pages from the end. The first tool makers and the ice ages fall on the last page. Neanderthal man and the cave artists are on the last line on that page. The first civilizations, such as Sumer, are within the last eight letters. Julius Caesar and William the Conqueror would coincide with the last two letters of the last word. Our own lifetime would be invisible. So short is human history compared with earth history.

There are still problems and uncertainties connected with the geological time scale, but the broad outlines are established and have on the whole been confirmed by various newly available methods of radioactive dating, notably by the Potassium-Argon method. Our diagram shows where the ice ages and man fit into the scheme of things.

What is an ice age?

The most obvious feature of an ice age is continental glaciation. In Europe, for example, an ice sheet like the one now covering Antarctica built up over Scandinavia. It grew in size until at one time, at its maximum, it covered southern Poland to the 50th parallel. In north America an even bigger ice sheet came equatorwards of the Great Lakes to the 40th parallel in places. But the ice sheets advanced and retreated many times. They would have reached this far south for no more than 200,000 years at the most, or two lines of the ice age page of our thousand page book. The milder intervals between glaciations are often termed interglacials. They were as warm as today, or warmer.

PLIOCENE

PLIOCENE
PLEISTOCENE

3m

7m

16m

10m

13m

18m

common
ancestor 20m

22m

24 million years ago

23m

21m

First stone
tools

6m

15m

12m

9m

2m

africanus

32

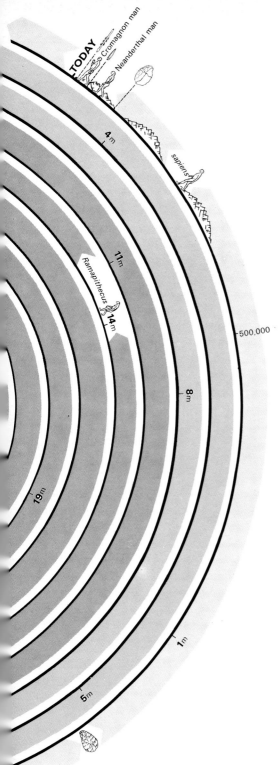

It was only about 10,000 years ago that man turned farmer, controlling a crop and settling in one place long enough to see it ripen.

For over 2 million years, 99 per cent of human history, man has been a hunter.

The mammal species ancestral both to man and ape lived about 20 million years ago. The first recognizable departure from that, along the hominid line, is betrayed by fossil remains of Ramapithecus, dateable to about 14 million years ago. Hominids africanus *and* erectus *then* Homo sapiens *including Neanderthal man and Cromagnon man followed at progressively shorter intervals. The earliest stone tools come from archaeological levels of some* $2\frac{1}{2}$ *million years ago. The subsequent long years of man the hunter's developing skill as stone tool-maker are 'the Palaeolithic' or the Old Stone Age.*

The later part of the Palaeolithic is marked by three great ice-advances, the last contemporary with prehistoric man's greatest technical and artistic achievement. This was the time when caves like Lascaux were decorated and when the barbed harpoon, the bow and the spear thrower were first devised.

In higher mountain regions, where the continental ice sheets have their origins, the snow line was much lower during a glaciation and valley glaciers descended further. Both valley and continental glacial extension imply lower temperatures, either only seasonally or on yearly average as well. However, without adequate nourishment from precipitation, especially from snowfall, ice sheets cannot form and most of Siberia, for example, was not covered by an ice sheet even at the height of European glaciation.

Did the ice sheets of Europe, America and the southern hemisphere all expand at the same time, and does a single pattern of temperature change fit all parts of the earth? One school of research has always favoured the view that this was so while other theorists, especially those who thought changes in the receipt of solar radiation caused the ice ages to come and go, expected different patterns in different parts of the world. Although it is not really known how closely the regions compare, at the moment the evidence supports overall similarity of temperature change.

Immediately outside the glaciated area would lie a belt of tundra; the other climatic belts would be compressed towards the equator. Temperate zones and their characteristic fauna and flora were pushed into southern-most Eurasia and north Africa. The subtropical zone contracted and the tropical zone was squeezed from north and south. Cooler temperatures prevailed on the equator and mountain ice caps grew—on Mount Kenya for example. Presumably there was less evaporation, and at times it was not so arid over much of Africa.

The Pleistocene ice age

The conception of an ice age is often attributed to Jean Louis Agassiz, a Swiss geologist, who promoted the idea in the 1830s, following suggestions by other pioneers in the preceding fifty years that former ice-action might be invoked to explain the presence of huge boulders far from their place of origin or to explain why moraines deposited by glaciers are to be found lower down Alpine valleys than the ice reaches today.

Meanwhile, in his *Principles of Geology* (1830–3), Lyell created the names Eocene, Miocene and Pliocene for three epochs of later geological time. But later geological strata were thinner and less continuous than those of previous periods and he decided to use their changing fossil content to identify the epochs. He noted that sea shells were among the commonest fossils and that the types found changed from level to level. Only from the Eocene onwards were any of these shells of types which survive today. On the other hand the fossil mammals of the Eocene were all extremely un-familiar types; not until the end of the Pliocene did surviving forms appear. Evidently the higher forms of life change faster.

In 1839 he proposed calling the epoch after the Pliocene 'Pleistocene'.

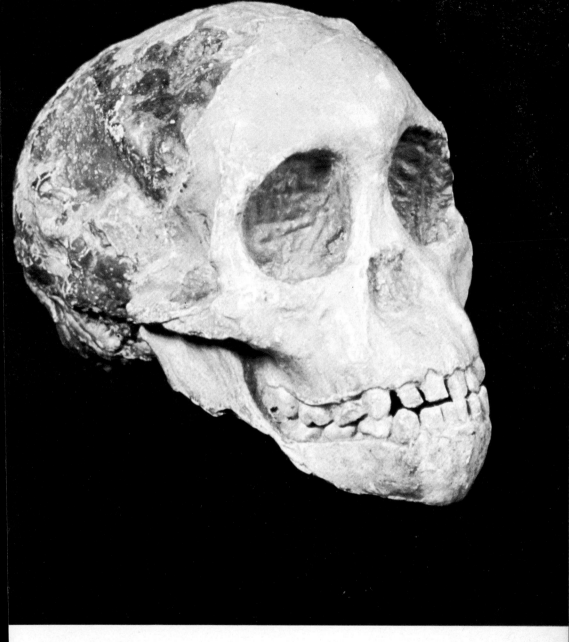

Juvenile skull found at Taung in Cape Province in 1924. The species Australopithecus africanus *was created to accommodate it.*

The savannah grassland of east Africa came into existence when the tropical rain-forests dwindled. It is probable that man first walked upright and first turned meat-eater and hunter in this region, exploiting the new opportunities offered by huge herds of animals grazing the plains.

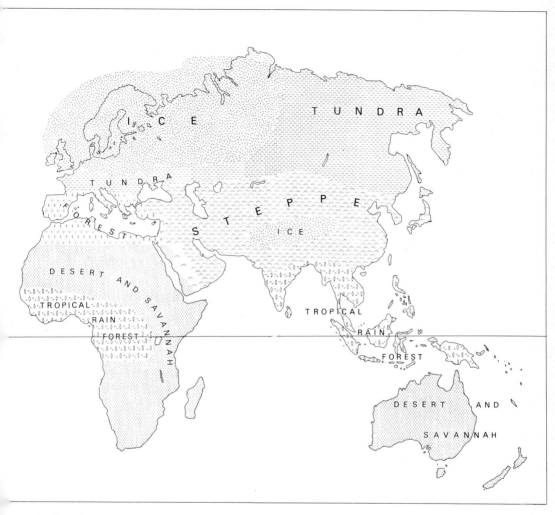

During the maximum extension of the ice sheets, tundra, temperate forest, grasslands and possibly also the tropical zones were compressed towards the equator.

37

It was to begin where the proportion of surviving forms of mollusca passed 70 per cent and where very few mammals were surviving species. It ended at the point where virtually all the mammals were 'recent' types.

It was Forbes who suggested that it would be desirable to equate Lyell's Pleistocene with the ice age and terminate them both at the same point in time. Ever since then opinion has been divided on whether faunal or climatic evidence best delimited and subdivided the Pleistocene.

The sequence of later geological deposits exposed on the coast of Norfolk and elsewhere in East Anglia was from the start prominent in Lyell's classification. It included three successive groups of deposits. At the top were the tills, representing several ice-advances over eastern England. Like the cave earths with their arctic animal forms, these obviously belonged to the ice age. Under the tills and close to sea level the Cromer Forest Bed was exposed, a silty deposit in which whole tree-stumps were occasionally found. At least part of this represented a warmer climate period than the tills above. Under the Forest Bed lay the shelly sands and silts known colloquially as the 'Crags'. These deposits blanket eastern Norfolk to a depth of up to forty metres in places, and contain fossil mammals such as the mastodon and extinct gazelles. Surviving types of shells ranged from 69 to 82 per cent of the total shells according to Lyell. Some of the Crags had indications of cold climate but not of an actual glacial advance.

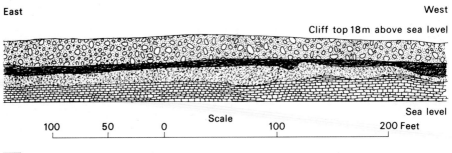

East

West

Cliff top 18 m above sea level

Scale

Sea level

100   50   0   100   200 Feet

Till: clay and other debris deposited during an ice-advance.

The Cromer Forest Bed includes plant remains indicative of warm climate.

Crag: shelly sands including, at some levels, fossil sea-shells indicative of cold climate but no actual ice-advance.

Chalk.

Deposits exposed in the cliffs of the Norfolk coast, near Cromer, belong to the 'ice ages', to use the term in its wider sense, but an actual ice sheet covered England only in the time after the Cromer Forest Bed.

Above *Thick sheets of ice, like this one now covering Antarctica, blanketed much of north America and northern Europe during the ice ages.*

Right *Rocks at Val Camonica near the foot of the Italian Alps were scraped and grooved by glaciers of the ice ages extending down into the Po valley.*

It is far from apparent where the ice age began in the Norfolk sequence and therefore, on Forbes' definition (equation of the Pleistocene with the ice age), difficult to tell where the Pleistocene began. On Lyell's original definition (more than 70 per cent of recent shell types), as well as on the most widely used modern definition, the Pleistocene began within the Crags.

The next main problem concerned the number of glaciations and whether they had been separated by warm periods (interglacials). It took over half a century to establish that there had been multiple glaciations in such areas as the Alps, the north European plain, Britain and America.

Unfortunately, earlier cold periods are mainly without direct evidence of ice-advance and cannot really be called glaciations. Nor can the warm periods between them justifiably be called interglacials. Nor are either of these terms fully appropriate outside the glaciated areas. Eventually one technique, the study of vegetational history by pollen analysis, made possible the reliable identification and synchronization at least of the warm periods vital to understanding of the Pleistocene.

Pollen analysis and vegetational history

Pollen is released into the air by most land plants and travels anything from a few metres to hundreds of kilometres depending on wind strength. Part of this pollen 'rain' falls on accumulating sediments and is preserved. The surface of a bog or the bed of a lake will provide ideal circumstances for this preservation. So hard is the outer shell of the tiny pollen grains that they are only destroyed by highly alkaline sediments or by the chemical process of oxydation.

Small quantities of sediment taken from an exposed section or from a borehole at close intervals upwards through a deposit will contain a record of the changing pollen rain. Under the microscope (for the grains are under 0·03 millimetres across) the pollen of plant types like oak (*Quercus*), pine (*Pinus*), hazel (*Corylus*) or grasses (*Gramineae*) can be identified. Unfortunately it is often difficult to tell the species. Evergreen and deciduous species of oak would indicate rather different climates.

Lennart Von Post, the Swedish botanist who pioneered pollen analysis in 1916, showed how the plant types whose pollen was present in a sample, and their frequencies, could be read upwards through a diagram to reveal a changing vegetational history.

Results accumulated from different areas were amazingly consistent. The lower layers of the peats and silts which overlay the moraines of the last glaciation had low frequencies of tree pollen along with tundra plants like the mountain aven (*Dryas octopetala*). Over this, birch and pine forests developed. Later on, oak and other deciduous forest trees dominated. This kind of pattern was revealed all the way from Ireland in the west to Poland and Russia in the east and clearly represented the normal vegetational history of the post-glacial period.

A surprising confirmation of the value of the technique came with radiocarbon dating. Pollen analysis reveals stratigraphic boundaries where one vegetation type replaces another. One might have expected the replacement of one type of forest by another to have been later in some areas than in others—the replacement of birch by pine for example. In fact the radiocarbon ages of these boundaries in different areas are so close that we are not even sure if there is a time lag between them.

Deposits of the last interglacial, at Herning in Jutland, substantially earlier than the post-glacial deposits we have been discussing, were investigated by pollen analysis as early as the 1920s. But it was not until after 1945 that similar investigations of interglacials began in earnest and a series of successive temperate phases of the Pleistocene began to be studied in Holland, Germany and elsewhere.

The pioneer investigator of the sequence of temperate periods in Britain was Richard West, now Professor of Botany at Cambridge University. West applied pollen analysis to the sequence of East Anglian deposits discussed above and disclosed no less than six distinctive temperate periods separated by cold periods—one of the longest sequences of its kind.

Work began in 1951 at Hoxne, where, a century and a half before, Frere had made such far-reaching observations. In sections and boreholes West studied a series of organic muds and even true peat lying on top of a thick chalky boulder clay or till left by an ice sheet. The large hollow in which the lake muds had formed was probably a 'kettle hole' formed by the melting of a gigantic block of ice caught up in the till. Clearly the lake had silted up in a temperate period, immediately after a major glaciation. A subsequent cold period was indicated by the overlying contorted gravels, of a type called solifluxion, formed over permanently frozen ground.

Analysis of pollen samples collected from over six metres of deposits revealed a vegetational history with some analogies to the post-glacial. But it had a number of distinctive features as well as evidence of a cooling climate at the end.

West called this temperate period the Hoxnian. When it was in due course compared with the vegetational history of other sites in Britain and on the Continent, one group, including Hoxne, exhibited a set of consistent features. West concluded that different vegetational histories represent different periods and that sites with a vegetational history of Hoxnian type all belonged to a single period. He took the view that this was an interglacial earlier than the last interglacial and equivalent to the Holsteinian of continental Europe.

One of the Hoxnian's most distinctive features was the presence of quantities of a water fern, *Azolla filiculoides*. This is found neither in the post-glacial vegetation of Europe nor in the last interglacial, and today it is a native only of America. Silver fir (*Abies*) is abundant in the pollen rain of one stage of the Hoxnian; like *Azolla* it is absent from the subsequent vegetational history of Britain. In addition yew (*Taxus*) was fairly common in the middle part of the Hoxnian, while another distinctive feature was that the tundra phase immediately preceding this Hoxnian interglacial supported quantities of sea-buckthorn (*Hippophae*).

In the hope of characterizing another temperate period West turned his attention to some lake deposits just outside Ipswich. This site gave its name to his Ipswichian, or last interglacial equivalent to the Eemian interglacial of continental Europe. The Ipswichian had features which distinguished it from the Hoxnian, post-glacial and other temperate periods: for example, the second half of the Ipswichian had very high frequencies of hornbeam (*Carpinus*).

The Hoxnian and the Ipswichian remain the only two temperate periods definitely known in Britain since the Cromer Forest Bed. Two earlier temperate periods are known to be recorded in the Cromer Forest Bed and two earlier still in the Crags below, as sampled in a borehole at Ludham on the Norfolk Broads. This number of alternating warm and cold periods caused little surprise, since parallel investigations in Holland, mainly by Waldo Zagwijn, had revealed a similar number; to date, in fact, the Rhine mouth sediments have revealed seven in all: two pre-Cromer temperate periods, three Cromer and two post-Cromer. Evidence from central Germany suggests that there should be at least two more post-Cromer temperate periods between the Hoxnian and the Ipswichian making a total of at least nine. Similar suites of temperate periods are known elsewhere.

The Cromer and later temperate periods have a distinctive four-part structure. Tundra-like conditions with little tree pollen gave way at the start of the interglacial to birch and pine forests as in the post-glacial. At the end of this stage, which West called stage I or pre-temperate, closed deciduous forests came in and the climate must have been about as warm as today. After the temperate stages, the return of pine and other conifers to dominance marks the lowering of temperature of the post-temperate stage (IV) and this was usually followed by evidence of glacial advance or tundra-like conditions. The main temperate division was further divided into an early temperate (II) and late temperate (III) stage; the latter included characteristic late arrivals like hornbeam and often an indication of thinning of the forest.

The pre-Cromer temperate periods seem to lack a clear 'late arrivals' stage III, even though the first of them (Zagwijn's Tiglian) seems to be very long. Hickory (*Carya*), Asian wingnut (*Pterocarya*) and hemlock spruce (*Tsuga*), along with other trees now extinct in Europe, are increasingly common as one goes back before the Cromer time.

Pollen analysis is bound to remain the key method of identifying

Above *To judge from the spores which are found,* Azolla filiculoides *was a common water plant during the Holstein and earlier temperate periods between ice-advances. But in the last interglacial it was missing and today it is found native only to America.*

Below *Pollen grains of silver fir (*Abies*), hazel (*Corylus*) and lime (*Tilia*) from the Hoxnian interglacial period. They are all under a tenth of a millimetre across but very distinctive in shape. In Britain, silver fir is typical of the Hoxnian but not of later periods.*

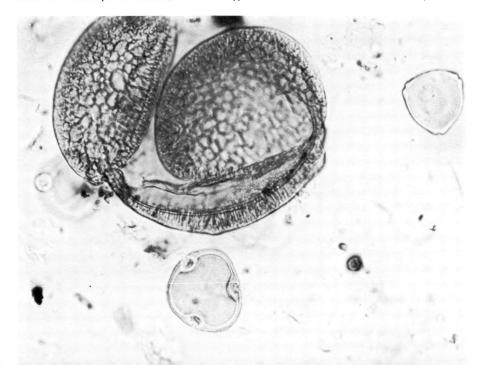

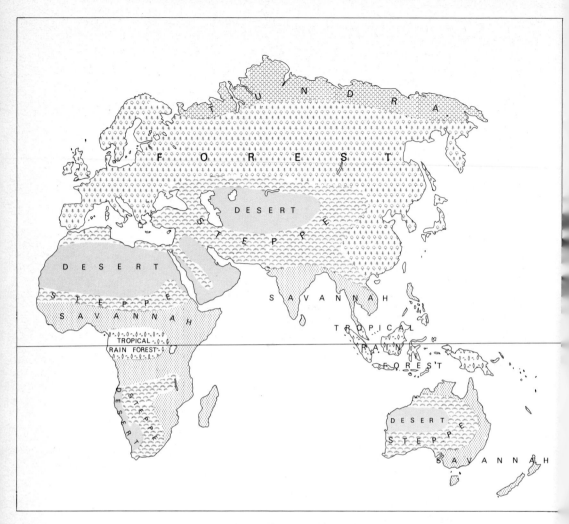

During the milder, interglacial periods, the climatic zones were probably in much the same position as they are today.

temperate periods until some other technique gives a similarly impressive framework of periods and climatic change.

On the Continent there is clear evidence for three main complexes of glacial tills separated by the two post-Cromer temperate periods—the Elster, Saale and Weichsel complexes. Evidence of earlier cold periods separating the long sequence of temperate periods is not in the form of tills but usually from tundra-like vegetation, or from frost wedges, solifluxion and other permafrost phenomena.

Dating from mammals

While plants and invertebrates have hardly changed at all since the Cromer Forest Bed many mammals of Europe have undergone a transition or died out; three-quarters of the species in the Forest Bed are now extinct while only about a quarter of the mammals of the two post-Cromer interglacials have disappeared. This is a classic example of Lyell's law that higher life-forms like mammals change faster than simpler forms like mollusca, plants and protozoa.

The change from a quarter to three-quarters of living species which marks off the Cromer faunal stage from the post-Cromer (main ice age) faunal stage is due to three factors: transition to new forms, arrival of species from elsewhere and extinction of old forms. The transition to new forms, the process most valuable to us in dating, is sadly rare; in any case the change is so gradual that over a period of many thousands of years transitional forms cannot usually be distinguished from the mother or daughter species. Most of the latest species transitions we know of are located late in Cromer or early in post-Cromer times. The evolution of the extinct genus of water vole *Mimomys* (with deep rooted teeth) into the modern genus *Arvicola* (with almost rootless teeth) apparently happened quite suddenly in late Cromer times.

The cave bear descends via three known ancestral forms, the approximate date of whose transition is known, the last one living in late Cromer times. The mammoth too has three known ancestral forms, its last transition contemporary with the Holsteinian interglacial.

The evolution of the horse is complex. The arrival of the earliest 'caballine' horse marks the beginning of the pre-Cromer Villafranchian. It evolves through a species of Cromer age into a type essentially the same as both the wild and domestic horses of recent times. The horse contemporary with the cave artists, as illustrated at Lascaux for example, is a small variety, very like Przewalski's horse of the Asiatic steppes.

It is partly from our knowledge of species transitions that certain distinctive types of elephant and pig are becoming extremely important in comparing the ages of African sites like Olduvai, East Rudolf and Sterkfontein.

Above *The horse which figures in prehistoric cave art, as at Lascaux, is a small variety, not very different from the wild type found in Siberia today.*

Left *200,000 year old fossil shells from Swanscombe (*Theodoxus serratiliniformis*) have a characteristic black zigzag pattern. It is unusual for the natural pigment to survive this long. The species is now extinct.*

Dating by successive strata: loesses and sediments
A common deposit of the ice ages was a fine wind-blown dust called loess. The loesses of northern France are claimed to represent cold dry 'glacial' periods and are divided into the younger (pale coloured) loess with three subdivisions belonging to the last glaciation, and the older (darker) loess of the preceding glaciation. The top of the older loess is weathered and reddened to some depth; on top of this lies the younger loess which is subdivided by minor soils.

Cave sediments in France may also have formed almost exclusively in periods of cold climate; the majority of them belong to the last glaciation. A few caves, such as Combe Grenal, have a major weathering horizon separating the last glacial deposits from those of the preceding glaciation.

Loesses and cave sediments are found widely across Europe but those found in France are particularly useful in dating the Palaeolithic.

Dating and terraces
The slow shaping of the landscape, especially by the changing routes and down-cutting of rivers, can help us date the Pleistocene. We can often detect flat, former river beds called terraces beside modern rivers. In the vicinity of mountain glaciers a distinct alternation occurs. During a cold period, much coarse debris and glacial material clogs up the width of the river valley; then in a subsequent warm period the river flows freely and cuts down, leaving the glacial gravels as a terrace.

The most famous scheme of names for Pleistocene glaciations, proposed by Albrecht Penck, was based on the glacial terraces and plateau gravels of the tributaries of the Danube which flow out from the Alpine valleys and glaciers across Wurtemberg and Bavaria. The lowest, most recent glacial terraces and the last glaciation with which they were equated were named Wurm, after one of the tributaries. The next terrace up was claimed to represent a Riss glaciation. Plateau gravel at a third level was Mindel, and a higher plateau gravel was Gunz, the earliest of Penck's glaciations. These names have been, and continue to be, very widely used though unfortunately in more than one sense (for example as a label for a time period), leading to regrettable confusion.

One of the most complete sequences of terraces is found in the Thames valley. As well as possible glacial terraces, some of the levels are clearly marine, left during warm periods of high seas. By 1939 S. W. Wooldridge had been able to show how the most extensive glaciation of southern England had diverted the course of the Thames past London.

Wooldridge divided the erosional and terrace levels into three stages. Stage I consisted of two high-level spreads of gravel, both believed to be left by gigantic arms of the sea flooding most of the London basin. The higher, 180 metre (600') Netley Heath gravel had marine shells like those of the early crags, and is of pre-Cromer age. The gravel was possibly left by the high seas of the first interglacial warm period. The 130 metre (430') Pebble (or Bushey) gravel can be linked from similarity of contained rock types to the East Anglian Westleton beds of Pastonian (early Cromer) date.

Wooldridge's stage II terraces all contained abundant 'Bunter' sandstone pebbles, brought from the Midlands by the Thames flowing across the Chiltern barrier through the Goring gap. As many as seven terraces have been distinguished, mostly dipping gently towards the east. Lacking fossils, they are difficult to correlate, except with the ice-advances. First, the river flowed past St Albans and across Essex into the North Sea via the region of the Blackwater. Then the river was diverted south past Finchley, whence it flowed north-east to its old route across Essex. The diversion was probably caused by the Chiltern Drift ice-advance, the oldest known in Britain. But a yet more important intervention of ice, the maximum, or Lowestoft, glaciation of the Anglian cold period, blocked the Finchley gap and sent the Thames on its present course past London.

The stage III terraces of the middle Thames are not easy to equate with those of the lower Thames around Swanscombe, where King and Oakley had worked out a very complete sequence by 1936. We can recognize the last interglacial terrace at Ilford and Crayford, and follow it upstream past Trafalgar Square and Brentford to the middle Thames where it forms the upper flood plain terrace. Recently I have been able to show that the archaeological sequence in the middle Thames Lynch Hill terrace corresponds with the Swanscombe (100' and interglacial) terrace of the lower Thames. Hoxnian fossil mammals and molluscs are abundant at Swanscombe.

Archaeologists and geologists have a lot to learn from sequences of river terraces like these which can put a long chain of events in their correct time order.

Dating in years
There is little doubt that dating in years, sometimes called absolute dating, is desirable, and if it could be done reliably and universally it would probably replace the relative sequences discussed so far. In fact it can only be done on a minority of deposits, and only in some cases can the results be trusted.

There are two main groups of chronometric (or time measuring) methods: those based on radioactivity and those based on simpler processes such as the record of passing summers and winters in tree rings and silt layers. Other methods not based on radioactivity have so far been little used. For example the volcanic glass, obsidian, suffers a chemical alteration of its surface, the depth of which is believed to measure the passage of time; so far it has had little bearing on the ice ages. The accumulation of fluorine in bones, known for a long time as an indication whether fossil bones can have come from the same deposit, has given dates for the four main interglacials, though these are dubiously based and widely neglected.

A very recent technique, based on a biochemical process, is racemization, or reverse of coiling in amino acids, in the surviving organic fraction of fossil bones. This apparently takes place at a consistent rate. So far we have only a few tentative dates going back to 300,000 years, but if the method proves reliable it definitely will be by far the most appropriate way of dating fossil men more than fifty thousand years old.

Varves and other annual sediments
The number of annual silt layers in an interglacial deposit can indicate its duration. Normally annual silt layers are counted back from the present or from a known point in time. The most important are those known as varves. A retreating ice sheet leaves behind long ridges of moraine or debris at its margin and the melt water of each summer ponds up against these to form 'proglacial' lakes. The lake remains until the moraine belt erodes through. By that time the retreating ice will usually have left new belts and lakes.

Each summer, silt builds up on the bed of the lake. In the winter, however, the lake freezes over and excludes new silt. Instead, very fine (clay grade) particles slowly sink to the bottom and form a thin dark layer. The silt and clay layers together form a varve and represent one year. Besides proglacial lakes, any lake that freezes over regularly each winter will leave annual sediments.

A Swedish scientist, Baron de Geer, worked indefatigably at the end of the last century to study and count the varves formed by the retreat of the last ice age. Counting for hundreds of kilometres along the line of retreat, he was able to correlate the various counts by matching distinctive patterns of thick and thin rings. The deepest varve close to a moraine in a proglacial lake roughly corresponds to the year of retreat from the moraine belt. Not without great difficulty and some uncertainty, this immense series of varves was finally linked to a point in recent historical time, a lake drained in 1796.

By 1912, and long before any other method of dating in years was available, de Geer was able to announce 'a geochronology of the last 12,000 years'. He dated the retreat from the Fennoscandian moraine, which coincides with the usual conception of the beginning of the post-glacial, to about 8150 BC. His Finnish colleague, Matti Sauramo, working independently on the other side of the Baltic, arrived at a date of 8200 BC. The best varve figure now available is about 8300 BC while radiocarbon gives a result within 100 years of this.

Perhaps the most neglected fact about varve dating is that it provides estimates for three earlier retreat stages of the last glaciation: the Pomeranian, Belt and Langeland moraines. The date for the Pomeranian is about 14,000 BC. If this figure is correct, the maximum extension of the last glacial ice in northern Europe is a little earlier than this, presumably around 20,000 BC.

Cases are known, at Marks Tey in England and at Munster in Germany for instance, where the number of annual silt layers indicates the duration rather than age of an interglacial. At Marks Tey the silts were made up of apparently annual laminations. A count suggested that the first half of the interglacial was not much over 15,000 years long and not under 6,000. Twenty to forty thousand years seems a good estimate of the duration of the whole interglacial.

Tree ring dating

Tree rings were also under investigation at the turn of the century. They have a certain amount in common with varves in that a thicker ring of vigorous growth cells forms during the favourable growing season; these are separated by thin dark rings of small cells of the unfavourable period. Sequences of several hundred tree rings are correlated with each other like varves.

Dating by tree rings, or 'dendrochronology', received a great boost when it was discovered that a little tree growing in the White Mountains of California, the bristlecone pine, was much older than any tree previously investigated. Hitherto it had been assumed that the giant redwood (Sequoia), with ages up to 3,000 years, was the oldest. One particular specimen of bristlecone pine, named Old Methuselah, was found to be over 4,600 years old. Charles Wesley Ferguson, who was investigating them, discovered that the hillside had some older trees, which, though dead, were well preserved. The record, already pushed back beyond 4000 BC, is being extended.

Tree rings on their own can be used for dating logs or timbers in buildings, as for example in the Pueblo indian villages of Arizona, which have survived 2,000 years in an arid environment. The method also offers a possibility of checking radiocarbon dating and has revealed a discrepancy of varying amounts between the two methods. For example, at 500 BC it is only about ten years while at 5000 BC it is nearer a thousand years. This is believed to have been caused by the increased radioactive carbon in the atmosphere at this time, in turn due to the concurrent weakness of the earth's magnetic field.

Radiocarbon dating

For the study of prehistoric events of the last fifty thousand years or so, it is impossible to over-emphasize the importance of radiocarbon dating; this span includes the cave artists, later Neanderthal men and much else besides.

The basis of the method is the known fact that all living matter absorbs carbon, by means of the carbon cycle. A tiny but consistent proportion of the carbon absorbed, less than one part in a million, is of the radioactive carbon (C14) caused by cosmic radiation in the upper atmosphere. The proportion in contemporary living matter is very consistent: one gramme of carbon gives off a radioactivity, as measured by a Geiger counter, of about 15·3 clicks or disintegrations per minute. This radioactive component behaves as all radioactive substances are known to, namely it breaks down by disintegration 'exponentially'. That is to say, once we know how long it takes for half of the radioactivity to disappear, we know that a quarter will be left after twice that 'half life', an eighth will remain after three 'half lives', a sixteenth after four, and only $\frac{1}{256}$ after eight half lives. The half life, as we shall see, is between five and six thousand years.

To turn this principle into a dating method requires only a reliable way of measuring the remaining radiocarbon in a sample of old carbon from an organism living at the time to be dated. By now hundreds of laboratories will attempt to do this and give a radiocarbon date. The best samples are charcoal, wood or burnt bone. But materials as diverse as ice and iron have been dated.

Because the method is now so widely used and so routine a part of archaeology, it is the possible sources of error which need stressing. It is not generally appreciated that up to a third of all dates have to be rejected as impossible, sometimes but not always due to a known source of error.

The possibility has to be considered that the level of radiocarbon varies over time or across the world. In fact we know that during atomic bomb testing in the 1950s the level became abnormally high, but at the same time we learnt that it quickly stabilized out to its new level all over the world. During the nineteenth century and up to about 1945 the level was low for it was being swamped by the quantities of non-radioactive carbon released into the atmosphere in the form of coal and other smoke, consequent on the industrial revolution. We are now able to some extent to document its variation in level at earlier times. A pilot test of the last 1,500 years carried out on Sequoia tree rings suggested that the errors would be small; each tree ring should have its own radiocarbon age, as only the outermost ring at any time is absorbing fresh radiocarbon. More extensive research, using the rings of bristlecone pine, showed that before 1000 BC the level of radiocarbon was high and dates were accordingly coming out too low. By 5000 BC dates were nearly a thousand years too low.

The extent of these errors depends on which half life is used. By convention all dates are calculated on the basis of 5,568 years, the first estimate made by Willard Libby, the inventor of the method. A higher figure, 5,730 years, is now believed to be nearer the truth; but now we know the C14:C12 ratio has changed, no one value will always be right. We can best continue to use the conventional value and develop a correction table for the whole span of the method. Uncorrected dates are sometimes expressed as 4500 bc as opposed to 4500 BC. Conversion values before 6000 BC are not yet available, but there is a hint from varves in Sweden and Minnesota that the error is less than a thousand years at the end of the last ice age.

Contamination of samples is probably the biggest source of error. A bit of coal mixed in a 500 year old wood-ash sample could put the apparent date back thousands of years. For samples over ten thousand years old the problem is reversed. Tiny particles of recent carbon, in the form of rootlets or humic acid, rejuvenate a date dramatically. A mere 0·02 per cent of recent carbon in a 64,000 year old sample will make the date 6,000 years too young. In this time range, because of the difficulties of removing the last traces of contamination, the highest of a series of dates is usually closer to the truth than the others; the scatter of a series of dates on a 60,000 year old sample would extend further towards the lower end (the present day) than towards the higher end (70,000 years ago). Although 70,000 years is often quoted as the limit of the method, for most laboratories it is more like 40,000.

Obviously there is a limit to how accurately a sample can be measured. For this reason most dates are only quoted to the nearest ten years, e.g. 5,310 years. Also a plus and minus figure (the standard deviation σ) is quoted. This should estimate that the true date has a 2 in 3 chance of falling in the bracket. It is far from clear if all laboratories estimate this bracket in the same way and it makes no allowance for contamination or simple mistakes in the laboratory.

Potassium-Argon dating and palaeomagnetism

Potassium-Argon dating has proved to be the main method for dating the geological time scale; though a few extra key dates come from the Rubidium Strontium method. Radioactive Potassium 40 breaks down into the gas Argon 40 whose half life is a mind-boggling 1·3 thousand million years. This is as clearly too long for ease of dating the ice ages as radiocarbon is too short. Even if the laboratory will date samples under half a million years, which few did until recently, the big problem is that Potassium 40 is not present in many archaeological or geological contexts. Most samples are volcanic rocks which trap the argon as it forms. The laboratory extracts the argon and measures it with a mass spectrometer.

Dating has gone ahead in some volcanic areas like east Africa and in parts of north America; but application to the best Pleistocene sequences has been slow and unsystematic. Dates for the European ice age span come only from the central Italian Latium volcanoes, and from the Laacher See volcanoes near Bonn, neither being closely linked with a good sequence. Volcanic eruptions in the earlier part of the ice age in the Auvergne have also been dated.

Volcanic rocks surprisingly record the magnetism of the earth at the time of their formation; it can be picked up with a magnetometer. In the 1960s the strange fact emerged that, on many occasions in the geological past, the earth's magnetism had been reversed. Compass needles would simply have pointed the opposite way.

A time chart of normal and reversed magnetization has been built up from lava flows measured by magnetometer and Potassium-Argon determination. For example, the current (Brunhes) period of normal magnetization began about 700,000 years ago; the preceding reversed (Matuyama) period went back to 2·5 million years ago, but had a few short 'events' of normal polarity in it. The application of magnetic reading to ocean sediments and even the sedimentary sequence of Holland is now being tried. But it looks as though the last reversal occurred in the Cromer period, a fact that does not help much in dating the main glaciations, which are more recent.

The uranium series

The largest series of isotopes belong to the uranium family. Uranium 238 has a half life close to the age of the earth ($4\frac{1}{2}$ thousand million years) and along with Uranium 234 and Uranium 235 it has been used for dating earlier geological events. Perhaps the strangest application is in 'fission track' dating. Each radioactive disintegration in Uranium 238 involves a small particle passing out of the rock in which the disintegrating isotope was present. In some volcanic rocks the tracks left by this fission can be recognized and counted; this is converted into a date, such as two million years for rocks at the base of the Olduvai sequence.

Two members of the uranium decay series, Thorium 230 and Protactinium 231, seem likely to help in dating the crucial period between 50,000 years, where radiocarbon leaves off, and about 400,000 years. Thorium 230, a daughter product of Uranium 234, has a very convenient half life of 75,000 years, while Protactinium 231, a daughter of Uranium 235, has a half life of 32,000 years. The breakdown of these isotopes has enabled dates to be calculated for samples of sediments from the ocean bed, stalagmite, sea shells and other substances. Recently it became apparent that fossil bone may be dated. This procedure assumes that in a few thousand years the bones incorporate their uranium but not the daughter elements thorium and protactinium. Subsequently, according to what is called the closed system model, neither uranium or its daughters migrate in or out of the sample and an age can be calculated.

In 1969 I submitted for dating some bone samples from British interglacial sites like Swanscombe and Clacton. The date for Clacton came out at 245,000 years with a generous plus or minus figure. It was the first such date to become available and it was exciting that it coincided so closely with my previous guesses of about 250,000 years. It is still too early to be confident of the results, but a quarter of a million years seems a good estimate for the Hoxnian interglacial and, as we shall see in the next chapter, for early *Homo sapiens.*

Ice age environments

The elements of the environment which changed substantially during the ice ages were temperature, precipitation, vegetation, soil and fauna. Each will ultimately need to be reconstructed for the different settings in which we find prehistoric man. Relief and sub-soil changed little either during or since the ice ages.

What was the extent of the change in environment brought about by the major glaciations? Ever since the pioneer excavators found numerous reindeer bones in the caves of the Dordogne, far from their present habitat, it has been questioned whether this area and others on the same latitude ever experienced tundra conditions. Arguing against tundra in the Dordogne, Hallam Movius and others have pointed out that its position on the 45th parallel of latitude, with an even annual distribution of sun, would preclude true arctic conditions. Secondly, Movius argues that the vegetation revealed in abri Pataud, one of the richer Dordogne shelters, was like that in the mountains of the Massif Central today rather than like tundra. He points out the presence of the garden dormouse in one ice age level, and notes that this does not live in regions with summer average temperature under 15°C. Movius rules out tundra or taiga, and envisages a climate like that near the tree line in the Massif Central. François Bordes, and others similarly opposed to the idea of tundra, held that the Dordogne experienced a kind of steppe environment of dry grassland in the cold periods.

In their simplest form the arguments for tundra down to the Dordogne are as follows. Cave faunas with an overwhelming dominance of reindeer, even in the summer, indicate tundra, so do the presence of musk-ox, Greenland seal and arctic fox. Many cave earths are made up of small angular blocks, which indicate a severe frost climate, and there is an absence of true soil formation; neither of these phenomena is found in the temperate zone, even in northernmost Britain, so they probably indicate tundra.

The climatologist's definition of tundra is that the mean July (=warmest month) temperature is under 10°C. At present the Dordogne is around 21°C, while south Wales, which was glaciated, has a July temperature of about 16°C, or 10 to 15° above the maximum temperature at which glaciation would be possible. More accurate figures for temperature depression are needed, but allowing a one to two degree reduction in the Dordogne

Above *Russian tundra, with the dwarf tree species whose pollen grains, when excavated in more southerly latitudes, suggest a once wider extent of this cold climate landscape.*

Below *Steppe grassland in central Europe. Most steppe has now been ploughed up, for it is the best agricultural land in the world.*

56

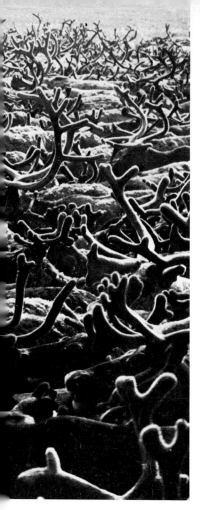

Left *Reindeer frequent the tundra. They eat lichens from the near-barren rock and actually shun warmer climates that bring the insect irritation to which they are very susceptible. They were the commonest prey of cave man.*

Far left *The bobak marmot is an animal of the Russian steppe; its fossil remains show that it ranged further west during the ice ages.*

Left *The arctic fox (*Alopex lagopus*) replaces the European fox in tundra regions. Rare examples of fossils of this species are found down as far as southern France in cave earths of the last cold period, a good indication of the former existence of true tundra in the middle latitudes.*

Above *The ibex today lives wild only in high mountain regions, above the tree line in the Alps for example. Its presence in the Dordogne in the ice ages shows how much lower the tree line has been at times.*

for the height of the plateau at 200 metres above sea level, tundra does seem probable, and for northern France certain. It must be made quite clear however that tundra in a middle latitude region like the Dordogne would be different from the arctic tundra of high latitudes.

The climatological definition of steppe is that evaporation exceeds precipitation. For mean annual temperatures under 10°C, this requires annual precipitation of well under 35 centimetres and probably under 20 centimetres. For the Dordogne, a maritime region with currently well over 50 centimetres, such a reduction has never been suggested and is rather improbable.

Steppe and tundra have a precise meaning for the soil scientist. True steppe is the invariable zone of the black earth or chernozem. These have been found as far west as Alsace as somewhat untypical fossil soils. They are unknown in western France. The so-called degraded chernozem, or prairie soil, may be present at one level in the loesses of the Paris basin but this level is just after the last interglacial and before the full glacial faunas appear.

The tundra is the zone with no true soil formation. Instead the permanently frozen ground tends to leave very distinctive traces in the form of frost distortions, such as polygon soils, frost wedges and cryoturbation, or frost disturbance. Although rare in southern France, features such as polygon soils have been found in the Dordogne, but the 'permafrost' was probably only sporadic.

Tundra for the zoologist would be characterized by the animals which live in present-day tundra: musk-ox, reindeer, arctic fox and hare and lemmings. There is no doubt that the remains of these are present in the glacial levels of the Dordogne caves. It is significant that, according to some authorities, the reindeer found in the caves are in some cases the barren-ground type, which live exclusively north of the tree line. The presence of the forest reindeer and occurrences of a mixture of tundra with woodland animals would be compatible with an environment resembling that at the boundary of tundra and forest.

The Dordogne and other southern French caves also reveal the bones of Alpine animals, like the ibex, chamois, marmot and snow vole, which live today above the tree line in the Pyrenees, Alps and other mountains. These are consistent with the view that altitudinally and latitudinally the tree line descended downslope and equatorwards to the Dordogne. The Alpine and tundra environments with their faunas would then have coalesced.

Because the steppe has been so extensively cultivated, little is known of its wild animals; they probably include Saiga antelope, suslik (ground squirrel), Bobak marmot, steppe lemming and pika. The Bobak is absent from the caves of western France, but the others are occasionally found in very low frequencies. Horses are grazers and would have flourished in steppe conditions. The very high frequencies of horse bones found at some sites indicate the absence of closed forest, which has insufficient grass, but are not evidence for true treeless steppe. The steppic element in the cave faunas is small.

The botanical characteristics of tundra are somewhat difficult to isolate since none of its plants is peculiar to this zone alone. Near-absence of trees is shared by tundra with steppe and desert. Dwarf tree species such as birch (*Betula nana*) and willow (*Salix herbacea*) are typical. Plant cover is sparse and lichens and mosses predominate. The recognition of tundra in the late glacial of northern Europe is from a low tree-pollen percentage and from the presence of light-demanding plants like the mountain aven or of dwarf trees. A steppe vegetation is dominated by grasses, and some other plants that would flourish in steppe—scabious, rock-rose and thrift for instance (*Knautia*, *Helianthemum*, and *Armeria*)—are found in pollen diagrams. It is not yet certain, however, what the precise incidence of plants is in the pollen record that proclaims true steppe.

It seems certain that during cold periods tundra-like conditions or actual ice covered the northern half of Europe and Asia. Steppe probably covered parts of eastern Europe near the Black Sea and the Caspian and was more extensive in western Asia and north Africa where it would tend to grade into the somewhat compressed zone of the savannah grassland.

Refuges of boreal coniferous woodland and even deciduous forests are believed to have existed in the extreme south of Europe, for example in southern Iberia, southern Italy and Greece, but the positive evidence for this is minimal.

The botanical question which is really at issue is where the poleward tree line stood in Europe at the height of the ice ages. The existence of tundra in southern Britain and Holland is not really in doubt. Was the tree line in Belgium, northern France or southern France? Tundra pollen diagrams are claimed from Belgium, north-east France and near Paris at L'Archet. Most surprisingly, late glacial tundra is claimed from Le Moura near Biarritz; even those who expect tundra in the Dordogne have wondered if there was a refuge of forest in the Biarritz region. So, until there is more evidence, the question of the position of the tree line is still open, but it is most unlikely that France was tundra-free.

The animals he hunted were the most important single element in the environment of ice age man. Bones of two animals are outstandingly abundant amongst the food debris of the later Palaeolithic—the reindeer of the limestone cave earths, and the mammoth of open camps across to Siberia. The reindeer first appeared in late Cromer faunas and became more common in each successive glacial period. Nowadays its natural habitat is the frozen north. The mammoth became extinct at the end of the last ice age, possibly helped by over-hunting. Other remains commonly found in ice age hunters' camps are the horse, the red deer, the fallow deer,

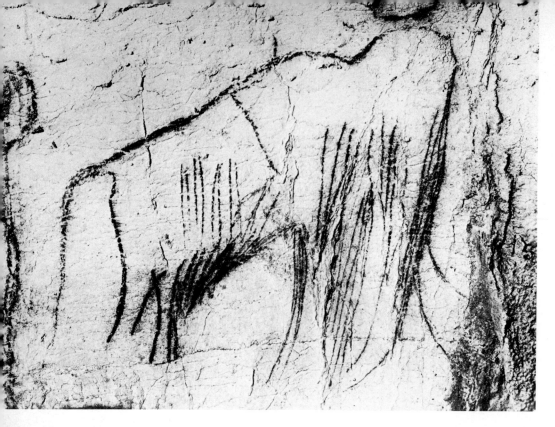

Above *The mammoth, meatiest animal available to the ice age hunters, probably lived mainly in tundra.* Below left *Hippopotamus bones found as far north as Trafalgar Square demonstrate the warmer climate of the interglacials.* Below right *The sitatunga (*Limnotragus*), inhabitant of reed swamps, indicates, when found as a fossil in such arid places as Olduvai, that the environment was once wetter there than it is today.*

60

Whole skeletons of the giant Irish deer have been found in Irish peat bogs dating from the end of the ice ages. The species is now extinct.

the ox and the bison. Also found are the cave bear, the woolly rhino, the giant Irish deer (*Megaceros*) (all three now extinct) and the elk.

The following, now extinct animals are typical of an interglacial: the straight-tusked or woodland elephant (*Elephas antiquus*) and two species of rhinoceros related to the living Sumatran form, *Dicerorhinus*. The most striking example of a European fossil indicating a formerly warm climate is the hippopotamus. Roe deer, wild boar, brown bear and rabbit were apparently at home in the milder climates of the interglacials.

As well as the case for an interglacial climate warmer than today, indicated, among the mammals, by the hippo for instance, there is corroborating evidence from shells, insects and plants. *Corbicula fluminalis*, a little mollusc, found in interglacial levels at Swanscombe does not now live nearer than the Nile valley. A beetle (*Oodes gracilis*) found in the last interglacial now lives in reed-swamps in southern Europe. Traces of vine in Suffolk and in north London suggest a formerly near-Mediterranean climate.

61

Environment of the tropics

The southern half of Asia seems likely to have had the most varied series of environments of any part of the Old World during the ice ages. It must have had steppe, desert, deciduous and monsoon forest, and the extent of tropical rainforest cannot have been much smaller than today. The actual fossil evidence for this is practically non-existent however.

In Africa, vegetation and type of environment vary primarily according to rainfall. Tropical rainforest gives way to savannah and ultimately to desert largely irrespective of any factor but rainfall. Only the environments of the extreme north and south fringes of Africa would have varied much according to temperature. Here there are two small zones of Mediterranean climate, which was presumably more extensive in cold periods. We know that there were also cold periods in Africa, for some of the few studies of vegetation change show that mountain vegetation zones shifted to lower altitudes contemporary with the last glaciation, and ice caps were bigger at this time.

A great deal of evidence has been put forward at different times for wetter (or more 'pluvial') climate in the past in Africa. For example there is the well-known claim that the Sahara was less arid and supported more vegetation. Unfortunately the evidence is very variable in quality and has all been disputed. But the question is of vital importance. At sites like Olduvai in Tanzania, we have good evidence of a former extensive lake, with rich vegetation supporting a large fauna that included the marsh buck (sitatunga), a swamp-dweller; today the area is arid. The now nearly dry lake Chad formerly covered hundreds of square kilometres. Other factors than rainfall, such as geological rifting, could have emptied these lakes. The lower temperatures would have reduced evaporation, and this alone would have led to the support of more vegetation; how much additional rainfall change is involved is not at all clear.

Changes in the size of the tropical rainforest, the original homeland of the primates, have a major bearing on human evolution. Fifty million years ago, long before man first appeared, rainforest covered most of Africa, not to mention most of Eurasia. The grassland was small and the deserts perhaps negligible. By Pliocene times, eight million years ago, the savannah had expanded greatly at the expense of the rainforest in which most primates lived. Some, like the baboons, joined the burgeoning game of the grasslands. Presumably man's ancestors made a similar choice.

Chapter III Apes and Human Ancestry

Man's place in nature

Man is, according to biological classification, a member of three successively more restricted divisions of the animal world, the vertebrates, the mammals and the primates. The primates are one of many orders within the mammal class of warm-blooded sucklers. Man belongs to the species *Homo sapiens*. A species is a group which by definition does not interbreed with another species.

Biologists classify species into higher groups such as the genus, the family and the order. They also believe that the member species of these groups had in the distant past a common ancestral species. The primate common ancestor probably lived about 70 to 100 million years ago, and by comparing the various different surviving primates we can deduce that it resembled a tree-shrew. All primates, including man, will be descended from him, but no birds or carnivores or whales, for example. Further back still the primates will share a common ancestor with the birds and even the fish.

The only lower primate ever to have been suggested as a close relative to man is the tarsier with its big eyes and agile fingers. Other authorities have suggested the monkeys of Africa and Asia, but most experts believe that these are not as closely related to us as the apes. Although Lamarck, the pioneer evolutionist of the 1790s, favoured the orang-utan, and a number of other experts have done so since, by far the most widely held view selects the chimpanzee and gorilla as our closest relatives, with the orang a little further away. The African apes were the choice of the Darwinians, an opinion confirmed by the most recent biochemical tests of blood and chromosome chemistry. It seems to be almost a dead heat between the two, with the chimpanzee perhaps a snout ahead. The best hope of reconstructing the common ancestor of man and chimpanzee is by analysing their physical similarities and differences.

Below *The chimpanzee normally walks on all fours, whereas man took to walking upright.*

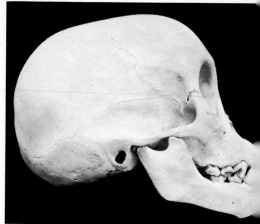

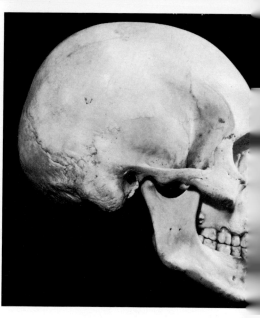

Above right *Juvenile chimpanzee skull.*

Below right *Modern human skull. Man's brain is bigger than his cousin the chimpanzee's, while his toothrow is smaller and without the projecting canine tooth.*

How does man differ from the apes?

Differences between man and ape begin with differences of posture and locomotion. Man walks upright on two legs. All apes however are primarily quadrupeds, and lack our balanced upright posture. The chimpanzee has an oblique posture, and long arms on to which he can easily fall before scuttling along on all fours. Closely related to this fundamental distinction is the nature of the hand. Apes' hands are similar to their feet and are used in locomotion, whereas our hands are useless in this respect. Freed from this function, the human hand has developed a better and more precise form of grip, with thumb and index finger in opposition. We also have excellent coordination of hand and eye.

Secondly the brain is to be considered. In terms of size alone man's brain is large. The average for the human brain volume is 1,350 c.c., with a weight of 1,350 grammes. A chimpanzee's brain averages about 350 c.c., and, though some gorillas' brains range up to 750 c.c., their average is much smaller. The human brain is also superior in its thicker cortex. Size alone is not the only factor, for whales and elephants have bigger brains. We need to take into account the factor that the smaller the ratio of body weight to brain weight the better. Man's body is only some fifty times as heavy as his brain. The chimpanzee weighs about 130 times its brain; and light bodied tree-dwellers like the gibbon and capuchin monkey equal or surpass us in this respect. By contrast the elephant is a thousand times as heavy as its brain and the whale eight thousand times.

The third main physical distinction between man and ape lies in the nature of the teeth and their supporting structure, the face and jaw. Man alone of the living primates has short, 'flush' canine teeth. Apes, monkeys and lower primates alike have long dagger-like canines which overlap with the opposite toothrow and interlock into it, preventing side to side mastication or grinding. A major corollary of this is that apes and monkeys with long canines have a gap in the opposite toothrow. Their teeth should not be crowded or the gap reduced or they cannot close their mouths. Humans characteristically have crowded teeth and gaps caused by tooth extraction when young will usually close up. Apes have a long palate with a more spaced toothrow, while we have a short palate and crowded toothrow. We are on the way to losing our last molars, the wisdom teeth, for there is no room for them. They are sometimes now congenitally absent. This apart, we have an identical tooth formula (2 incisors, 1 canine, 2 premolars and 3 molars) to apes and old world monkeys. American monkeys and lower primates have more teeth. Neither are human and ape teeth individually very different. The molars of both are believed to derive from the pattern found in a fifteen million year old ape; differences in the pattern of chewing surface are apparent only to specialists, and are almost indistinguishable on worn teeth. Ape teeth tend to be a bit larger than ours, but, as we shall see, fossil human teeth turn out to be larger than ape teeth.

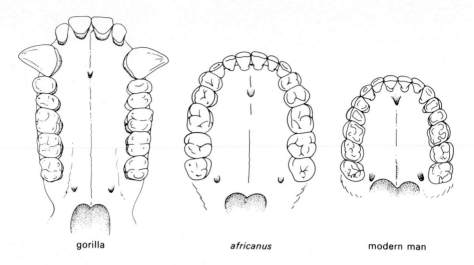

gorilla   *africanus*   modern man

The toothrow of the gorilla is longer than that of modern man or of Australopithecus africanus. *Its most distinctive feature, found in all apes but absent in all hominids and thus distinguishing their fossil remains, is the massive canine tooth.*

But specialists have not always agreed which of the human features came first.

Early this century prominent anthropologists, including Marcellin Boule and Grafton Elliot Smith, thought that the brain led the way in human evolution. Man first acquired a brain of modern size and shape, they thought, which led in due course to uprightness, human teeth and culture. They tended to expect that early fossil ancestors would be very like modern man; and fossils differing from us, such as Neanderthal man and especially *Australopithecus*, were politely but firmly placed on collateral lines as 'cousin species', destined to become extinct. The parallels with catastrophism have been noted by modern workers.

In the nineteenth century Darwin regarded upright posture as at least as important a human criterion, and Huxley, following an evolutionary viewpoint, predicted that our fossil ancestors would be found to be very different from ourselves, with an increasingly ape-like aspect in the past. This kind of view, which we now regard as correct, had been largely overshadowed in the first half of this century, to be revived since World War II by workers like Sir Wilfred Le Gros Clark and Sherwood Washburn. They have shown that upright posture and a modern dental pattern had evolved more than a million years ago. Java man, found in 1890–1, had a brain size of less than 1,000 c.c. but we are satisfied that he had upright posture and human teeth; indeed *Australopithecus*, living earlier still, had human posture and teeth but an even smaller brain.

Ironically some early fossil evidence favoured the brain-first theory.

The upper jaw of one of the earliest hominids, *Ramapithecus. The canine tooth is smaller than that found in fossil apes of the same period.*

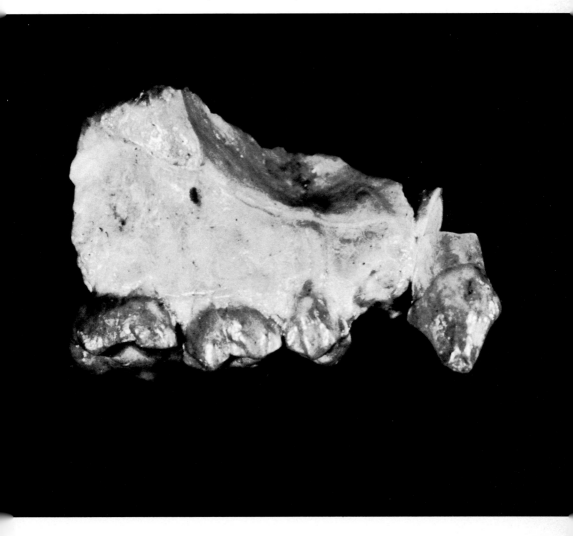

The notorious Piltdown pieces, announced in 1911, consisted of a skull of modern, big-brained type, with a jaw bone of ape-like appearance; both were believed to be ancient, and clear evidence for the brain-first theory. Meanwhile Boule was reconstructing his type specimen of Neanderthal man (from a cave in south-west France) with a big brain but a stooping posture. Again posture seemed less evolved than brain. But, as we now know, Piltdown was a fraudulent 'plant' with an orang's jaw, and Neanderthal was an erect biped and had been misinterpreted by Boule.

Today any of these three features, upright posture, enlarged brain or short canines, would be sufficient to class a fossil primate species as a member of the human family rather than an ape.

The first hominid

The earliest known trace of hominid features is in a fossil from Fort Ternan in Kenya. Here a hominid jaw has reduced canines and a short palate and toothrow. This is dated by the Potassium-Argon method to about fourteen million years ago, while a somewhat similar fossil from India is less closely dated, but is of much the same age. They are often regarded as both belonging to the genus *Ramapithecus*, which may be the first hominid genus and much earlier than *Australopithecus*.

So far we have not found enough of the skull of *Ramapithecus* to determine his brain size but most authorities expect it to be in the chimpanzee range, perhaps 300 to 400 c.c. Nor have we good evidence of his posture. Was he upright or still a quadruped like the apes? We should soon have the fossils to tell us. Meanwhile an attractive theory is that *Ramapithecus* was already a biped. Remember that at some stage he left the rainforest where he was probably used to semi-uprightness from climbing in trees. On entering the tall grass savannah, he may have made the transition to bipedalism. This would have freed his hands for improved manipulation. Using clubs for defence and sharp stones for cutting, he would have been able to manage without his dagger canines. A few rare mutants with small canines found they could chew from side to side and thus grind nutricious grassland seeds that had formerly not been edible. The molars turned into querns, and the toothrow without its dagger canines closed up into the human dental arcade of parabolic shape.

In the nineteenth century Darwin and his contemporaries were acutely conscious of the fact that no fossils had yet been found that were anywhere near half-way between man and ape. This was the basis of the popular idea of a 'missing link'. In the twentieth century we have numerous fossil hominids with features intermediate between man and ape; they are spaced out consistently over the last fifteen million years in such a way that there is no one major gap. The concept of a missing link is dead.

As fossil hominid remains accumulated the normal custom was to name each one a new species. Since a species is by definition reproductively distinct, this meant in effect that they were being placed on different diverging branches of evolution. Occasionally two species were seen as stages of the same branch, but it was usually made quite clear that this was not intended. A further consequence of coexisting hominid species is that, because only one species survives, all but one of them must belong to extinct branches—the 'cousin species'.

Branching is to be expected in the evolution of biological groups with limited distribution, limited mobility and a tendency to specialization. Groups within a species can branch only when they occupy separate territories and are isolated to the point where interbreeding ceases. This situation has to persist for thousands or even millions of years before the groups can diverge sufficiently to become a genetically separate species. Branching clearly occurred in the common ancestor of man and apes. But man's subsequent adaptation has made it increasingly unlikely for this to happen again: he has a wide, and latterly global, distribution; he is mobile as a hunter and few barriers prevent his spread and movement; he breeds readily and the long established practice of marrying outside the tribe means that he disseminates his genes more widely than most animals. Man's specialization is his lack of physical specialization and his commitment to culture. When man finds himself in challenging circumstances, he adapts his culture rather than his physique.

Nevertheless, there are special circumstances in which we would be forced to admit that hominid species might branch. The main requirements would be that two distinct hominid types should persist as fossils side by side over a long period in the same territory, that samples of each should indicate that one does not grade into the other, that differences between them should seem to be adaptations to particular ways of life and that there should be evidence for earlier isolation.

The alternative to a branching model of human evolution is a linear model. In a single, non-branching lineage over a long period of time we expect to detect changes in the form of improved adaptation to existing circumstances or readaptation to new circumstances. It has long been the custom to 'chop up' these lineages into evolving segments and give each one a species name. If we actually closely examined the arbitrary moment of of time when one species gives way to another we would obviously find some individuals who lived through this moment. Those who were born just after it would look very much like those who died just before it. More importantly, given the normal variability of a population (especially localized variation), it is common for one part of the population to have advanced further than others in the direction which overall change is taking. For this reason a backward part of the population after the species boundary will physically resemble the earlier species, just as an advanced part before the boundary would resemble the succeeding species. This leads to the pseudo-duplication of species in a lineage. Once the process is understood it should cause no surprise.

A belated realization of the shortcomings of a branching model of human evolution led an influential group of anthropologists, meeting at a conference in 1962, to adopt the linear model. While previously it had been thought more prudent to use a new species name for each new fossil hominid, the revised procedure was to put new fossils on a known line and in an existing species *unless* there was clear evidence to the contrary.

The 1962 simplified classification provisionally recognized four species: *africanus, robustus, erectus* and *sapiens*. The last two were placed in the genus *Homo*. *Homo sapiens*, modern man, originated about a quarter of a million years ago as represented by the Swanscombe skull. An ancestral species, *Homo erectus*, included Java and Peking man. The earlier hominid species, *africanus* and *robustus*, were placed in the genus *Australopithecus*.

A linear model of human evolution is in no way binding on scholars. Some, including the followers of the late Louis Leakey, have continued to favour an essentially branching model. But it is remarkable how widely the newly restricted list of four species has been adopted.

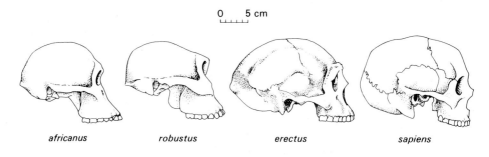

0   5 cm

africanus   robustus   erectus   sapiens

The four hominid species.

Early South African hominids

Detailed descriptions of the hominids found in South Africa before 1960 have now been published. Since they were the first to be validly named as species according to the rules in force in biology, new finds must be placed in this same species or be shown to be different. The South African finds are nevertheless poorly dated and their interpretation is difficult.

The first find was the child's skull discovered at Taung in northern Cape Province in 1924. This was the specimen for which the name *Australopithecus africanus* (southern ape of Africa) was created. The name *Australopithecus* was the genus name retained according to priority by the

70

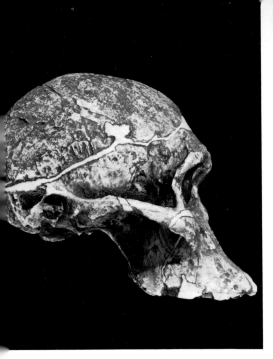

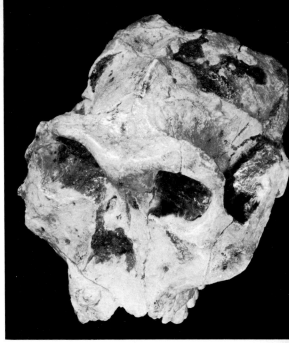

Above left *Adult* Australopithecus africanus, *from Sterkfontein.* Above right Australopithecus robustus, *from Swartkrans.* Below left *Leopard's tooth marks on a* robustus *skull from Swartkrans support the view that these hominid bits were accumulated by carnivores and that* robustus *was less likely than* africanus *to have become a carnivore and hunter himself.* Below right *The earliest skull from Olduvai (hominid 24) is the most complete of those attributed to* 'Homo habilis'.

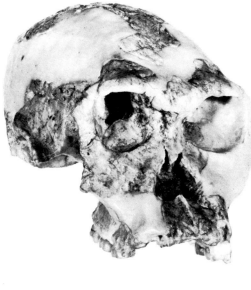

1962 conference on hominid species. The more recent discoveries, from 1936 to the present, have been made in the Transvaal, notably at three sites in the Sterkfontein valley near Johannesburg, and one further north at Makapan Limeworks.

The main Sterkfontein site has revealed numerous remains of a small hominid; altogether more than thirty individuals must be represented, though not many are at all complete. The current view is that the main Sterkfontein fossils are over two million years old. However, Taung may be more recent. Both are held to be representative of the gracile species *africanus*.

The Sterkfontein population was small-bodied; a pelvic bone suggested a weight of only 20–23 kilos (40–50 pounds). Stature was probably about 120 centimetres (under 4′). Brain size was small, certainly under 600 c.c. (compared with our 1,400 c.c) and one estimate puts all the brain cases between 400 and 500 c.c. The teeth by contrast were large; both molars and front teeth were bigger than ours, in spite of the tiny body size. A consequence of this was that the face was large and the front teeth protruded.

Most of the specimens seem to have been female; the body and brain size of the males could have been a lot bigger. The body to brain weight ratio however would have been similar, namely about 40 or 50 to 1 (22kg: 0·45kg). This is virtually the same as in modern man, and much closer to man than the chimpanzee ratio of 130 to 1.

Fossils from Makapan Limeworks are believed to belong to the same gracile species. The most recent view is that this is the oldest of the South African hominid sites and may be around three million years old; but such figures should not be regarded too confidently.

Some later deposits at Sterkfontein have yielded a few jaw pieces of what seems to be a more advanced gracile hominid. These may be $1\frac{1}{2}$ to 2 million years old. Stone tools, absent from the earlier sites, were found with them.

The name *robustus*, now often used for a robust species contrasting with the gracile species *Australopithecus africanus*, was originally applied to hominid fragments from Kromdraai in the Sterkfontein valley and the full name was *Paranthropus robustus*. Some workers like John Robinson say that *africanus* is a species of the genus *Homo*, like *Homo erectus* and our species *Homo sapiens*, but that *robustus* is not. The best known *robustus* population is from Swartkrans close to Kromdraai; it may date from $1\frac{1}{2}$ to $2\frac{1}{2}$ million years ago. Locally *robustus* is definitely later than *africanus*, but an advanced form of *africanus* seems to be roughly contemporary with *robustus* at Swartkrans itself.

The thirty or more individuals recovered in fragments from Swartkrans in 1948–52 indicate a bigger hominid species than *africanus*, weighing from 65–90 kilos (140–200 pounds). The brain size of the few determinable skulls is around 500–530 c.c. Again these estimates are on probable female specimens; the males could be bigger. The body to brain weight ratio is at least 100 and probably about 120 to 1; this is not very different from chimpanzees, and is a much less favourable ratio than in *africanus*. Stature may have been in the 140–150 centimetre ($4\frac{1}{2}'$–5') range.

What really distinguishes *Australopithecus robustus* is tooth pattern and the skull architecture which is related to the mastication performed by these teeth. The molars are truly enormous; they have in some cases nearly three times the grinding surface of modern human molars. But equally striking is the fact that the front teeth—incisors and canines—are smaller than in *africanus* and very much the same size as our own. The molars are scratched and chipped and evidently underwent much wear. The skull has enormous cheek bones, strong bony buttresses and a bony crest along the top of the skull. Robinson's explanation of these dental patterns is dietary. The *robustus* form ate vegetable foods and needed its big teeth to cope with the grit that was dug up with them. The *africanus* type was omnivorous and needed bigger front teeth for tearing at its meat. If the seed-eating theory discussed earlier is correct, *robustus* may be the end product of this adaptation, while *africanus* had adapted in a human direction towards omnivorism.

Some authorities have wondered if *africanus* and *robustus* belong to the same species, perhaps male and female, or belong to the ends of a big range of variation. Neither of these seems very likely. Another suggestion is that *robustus* is an evolutionary link between *africanus* and the later *erectus* species. The dental evidence does not seem to support this and they are anyway apparently contemporary in east Africa. So, at the moment, the front-running theory is that there have been two branches since before three million years ago, one leading to *erectus* and *sapiens*, the other to *robustus*.

As mentioned earlier, both types seem to have been upright bipeds. There is some evidence from the femur-head and foot of *robustus* that it was a rather less efficient form of biped. However, according to one view, scapula and clavicle bones in the *africanus* lineage indicate that in the not very distant past it was a tree swinger. It is possible that bipedalism takes a number of forms, and that neither hominid was very like us in walking. Certainly neither was very like any known ape.

Early east African hominids
The lower levels of the Olduvai Gorge site in Tanzania have revealed some fine hominids between 2 and $1\frac{1}{2}$ million years old. A robust form, Olduvai hominid 5, is sometimes given its own species. The skull is like *robustus* of Swartkrans but with even bigger molars and massive, bony, muscle attachments. Four important skulls of gracile type have been attributed to a new species *habilis*. Their brain sizes are 560 c.c., about 650 c.c., 640 c.c. and 620 c.c.; they thus fall neatly between *africanus* and *erectus*.

73

Such features as the brow ridges and other bony bars are variable, one having very pronounced brows and another having very reduced brows. The teeth are a little narrower than in *africanus* of South Africa. Posture was clearly erect as indicated by a surviving set of foot bones. These indicated a stature of just under 140 centimetres ($4\frac{1}{2}'$), so *habilis* was probably a little bigger than the South African form, with a nearly identical body to brain weight ratio. All this suggests that *habilis* was a late form, possibly a sub-species, of the species *africanus*.

Discovered in the 1970s, a series of over a hundred hominids from the east side of lake Rudolf in Kenya promise to become our best early hominid sample. Dated, like Olduvai, by Potassium-Argon determinations on the volcanic rocks, the East Rudolf deposits are $1\frac{1}{2}$ to 3 million years old. They include a good series of fossils of robust type, including one nearly complete skull and one possibly juvenile.

The remainder of the East Rudolf fossils are unlike *robustus* and resemble *erectus*, *habilis* and *africanus*. Two skulls, numbers ER1813 and ER1805 in the long list of fossil bones found at the site, belong to the time-range from 2 to $2\frac{1}{2}$ million years ago and have brain sizes of about 500 c.c. and 650 c.c. Like *habilis* these neatly span the gap between earlier *africanus* and later *erectus* populations.

The skulls which have attracted most attention are numbered ER1470 and ER1590; both are seemingly in the 750–800 c.c. range, not far below *erectus*, though in shape more like *africanus* or *habilis*. They are claimed to be earlier than a volcanic level of 2·6 million years old. This poses a dilemma to which the following answers are possible: they are only about $1\frac{1}{2}$ million years old and transitional to *erectus*; they are over $2\frac{1}{2}$ million years old and are part of the same lineage as *habilis* but a bit bigger; there are two lineages of gracile hominids before $2\frac{1}{2}$ million years ago, one (ER1470 for example) having a brain size of over 750 c.c., the other (like *habilis* or *africanus*) being smaller-brained and, though much more widely found, eventually dying out. Since *habilis* is a probable tool maker and grades into *erectus*, the first two options outlined above seem to be more likely.

Investigations in the late 1960s north of lake Rudolf in the Omo valley of Ethiopia revealed a series of hominid fragments, mostly teeth and jaws, that were between two and four million years old. Both robust and gracile forms are represented by teeth and jaws and similarities with the South African and Olduvai hominids can be detected.

Several other sites in Africa have yielded hominids similar to the robust and gracile lineages. Yayo in Chad Republic is the northernmost and is probably gracile. The best robust jaw is from Peninj in northern Tanzania. The gracile lower jaw found at Lothagam south of lake Rudolf is, at 5 to 6 million years of age, the oldest hominid fossil yet known apart from *Ramapithecus*. A tantalizing single upper molar from the Baringo area is about nine million years old but constitutes insufficient evidence for an attribution to *africanus* or to *Ramapithecus*, both of which it loosely resembles.

As of 1975 the most intriguing discoveries seem to be coming from the northern half of Ethiopia, in the Hadar basin near Dessye. This includes much of the skeleton of a three million year old hominid with a stature of only about 100 centimetres (3–3½'). And from Laetolil, near Olduvai, come jaw fragments of a hominid 3½ million years old.

Homo erectus

According to the linear model of human evolution we have been using, *Homo erectus* is the species which is ancestral to *Homo sapiens*, and descends from the gracile lineage of the early African hominids, The species name '*erectus*' comes from Java man, once believed by Eugène Dubois, the young Dutch doctor who first found him, to be a separate genus *Pithecanthropus erectus*.

The finds of the 1890s at Trinil in Java included a small flattened skull cap of about 900 c.c. and a femur which is strikingly modern in type. This was the first indication, bitterly disputed at the time, that the brain was still small and flattish when posture had become essentially human. Subsequently, at least six more skulls have been found in Java of similar age. The smallest is 775 c.c. and the largest 975 c.c.; they thus lie at and just below the extreme lower limit for modern brain sizes and bridge the gap to large gorilla brains. But the body weight was perhaps only a little below that of today, thus probably 60 to 75 times the brain weight—one of the poorest ratios found in humans. The femur suggested a stature of 168 centimetres (5½') but a slender build; clearly more evidence of the body would be useful.

The Java hominids come from two geological levels. The later level is associated with a collection of extinct animals of the 'Trinil' type, probably contemporary with the Cromerian, while the earlier level, with its Djetis fauna, may be pre-Cromer. This earlier level precedes the fall of a shower of tektites or small meteorites across south-east Asia which geologists have dated to about 700,000 years ago. The earlier Java men may thus have lived a million or more years ago. The later Trinil men lived perhaps about 700,000 years ago.

A more recent series of skulls from Ngandong on the Solo river near Trinil may be about 100,000 years old. They retain some features of earlier Java man, but show a considerable increase in brain size—1,035–1,255 c.c. Skulls from Australia of quite recent date, less than ten thousand years old, are remarkably similar to Solo and earlier Java men. They are usually classified as *Homo sapiens* with surviving *erectus* features, although Carleton Coon argued that Solo must be firmly classified as *erectus*. It is mainly a question of terminology; the similarity to *erectus* is however a fact.

The other fossil population used with Java man as the type material of the redefined species *Homo erectus* came from the Choukoutien limestone fissures, some fifty kilometres from Peking; it was found mainly in the 1930s. The brain size of five reasonably well-preserved skulls was 915 c.c. for a young person and 1,015–1,225 c.c. for the rest. The Peking people were a little shorter than the stature indicated by the Trinil femur, but probably stockier. One femur indicated a height of 158 centimetres (5′ 1½″), and the body weight was probably similar to present day, small people from eastern Asia (Ainu, Japanese etc.).

Pollen analysis has indicated that Peking man lived in a cold period; related faunal remains, which are late Cromer in type, suggest that this might have been during the first post-Cromer glacial advance. A date of 300,000 years ago obtained by the new amino acid racemization technique is consistent with this view.

A post-war *erectus* find is from Lantien in central China. With only 778 c.c. it is smaller brained than Peking man but compares well with Java man, with which it might possibly be contemporary.

Several European fossils have been tentatively attributed to *Homo erectus*. The lower jaw from Mauer near Heidelberg was found in 1907 with a fauna of perhaps 350 to 400 thousand years ago. An occipital fragment (back of the skull) sealed in a travertine deposit at Vertesszöllös, north of Budapest, with a very late Cromer fauna, has three uranium series dates averaging a little over 300,000 years ago. A fragment of tooth found just outside Prague may be human and is older than both these. The Mauer jaw, though massive, has smaller and therefore more modern teeth than any other *Homo erectus* fossil. The Vertesszöllös fragment, from a brain with a capacity of 1,250 c.c. to 1,400 c.c., also lies at the extreme upper end of the range of known examples of *Homo erectus*.

In Africa some jaws and a skull fragment from Ternfine in Algeria are usually attributed to *erectus*. But the best African *erectus* skull is hominid 9 from Upper Bed II at Olduvai. It may be about a million years old and its brain size is possibly about 1,000 c.c., but these figures have not yet been reliably fixed. Hominid 12, which is nearer half a million years old, from Bed IV of the same site, is a fragmentary skull but very thick-boned. Pelvic and femur pieces found with it are also attributed to *Homo erectus*. It is possible to regard the Olduvai hominids as a sequence leading into *Homo erectus*. Similarly some of the latest fossils from East Rudolf, the jaws designated ER730 and ER992, the skull fragment ER1466 and the femur ER737 may represent early *erectus* or a transitional form.

Later African skulls retain *erectus* features: the Saldanha skull from South Africa, possibly 100 to 200 thousand years old; the Broken Hill skull from Zambia, with a racemization estimate of 130,000 years; and Omo II

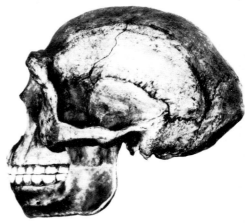

Above *A restored skull of 'Peking man', Homo* erectus *from Choukoutien, 50 kilometres from Peking.* Left *An attempt has been made by the Russian anthropologist Mikhail Gerassimov to add the soft parts to recreate Peking man's original appearance.*

Right *The fossil human skull from Steinheim, which, along with fragments from Swanscombe that are also some 250,000 years old, is now usually classified as early* Homo sapiens.

Next page *A skull found in 1971 in the Arago cave at Tautavel is probably early* Homo sapiens.

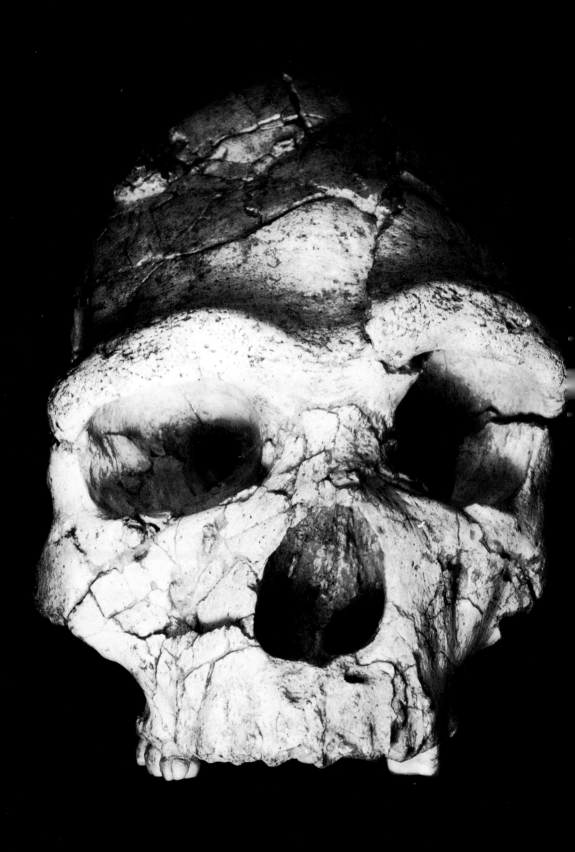

with uranium series estimates around 100,000 years. So, while Africa has few skulls from the true *Homo erectus* period, it has a fine series of early skulls leading into *erectus*, and plenty of evidence for survival of *erectus* features.

Early Homo sapiens

The term *Homo sapiens* refers to our own species but where this begins in the past is a matter of some debate. At one time the name was reserved for fossil men who were not significantly different from ourselves and who were later than Neanderthal man, that is, later than about 35,000 years ago. It is now more often used in a wider sense to include all humans since *Homo erectus*, commencing with the fossils from Swanscombe and from Steinheim.

These two skulls were by coincidence both discovered in the 1930s in western Europe and are of similar geological antiquity, namely 200,000 to 300,000 years according to uranium series dating. Strangely we have no European skulls contemporary with *erectus*, and, conversely, there are no Asiatic skulls known to be contemporary with Swanscombe or Steinheim.

The Steinheim skull, found near Stuttgart with a rich fauna in which *Elephas antiquus* predominates, is almost complete but badly crushed; no fully restored version has been made available. The Swanscombe parietal and occipital skull bones found in 1935 and 1936 were reunited with the second parietal in 1955 to make up the brain case though without the frontal part. They come from Barnfield pit, some 25 kilometres downstream from London and only about one kilometre from the Kentish foreshore of the Thames estuary. With them were found the remains of many mammals and molluscs as well as innumerable stone tools.

The 1962 conference on hominid classification favoured inclusion of these skulls in *Homo sapiens* for the following reasons. The Swanscombe brain size is estimated as at least 1,270 c.c., which is larger than any *erectus* skull. Steinheim is only about 1,170 c.c., and like Swanscombe seems to be a female skull. It is nevertheless larger than the largest female *erectus* known (Peking at 1,015 c.c.) but not larger than the Peking male, 1,225 c.c. The second reason was the shape of the brain cases which seemed to conform to the more rounded form of modern man rather than to the flattened, deflated shape of *erectus*. Carleton Coon stressed that *erectus* skulls seen from the rear have their sides sloping in to the top, while *sapiens* skulls are seen to be rounded or even puffy from this angle. The Steinheim teeth, and all later European hominid teeth, are smaller than the smallest in the *erectus* size range.

The inclusion of Swanscombe, Steinheim and their successors in the species *sapiens* has the effect of grouping populations with big brow ridges, like the Neanderthals and Steinheim, together with populations like Cromagnon and modern man in which the brow ridges are rarely apparent and the face is smaller and less protruding. These at first sight rather different types may be distinguished as neo-sapiens looking like modern man and palaeo-sapiens with big brow ridges.

Early accounts of the Swanscombe skull often implied that it was entirely modern in type, while Steinheim was a near-Neanderthal type, clearly belonging to a separate species and headed for extinction at the time of the latest Neanderthals. Subsequently an extensive metrical and statistical study by Joseph Weiner and Bernard Campbell showed that they were more similar to each other than to any other fossil skulls, or to any one of a large series of modern skulls.

The mistake made by those who wanted Swanscombe to be a skull of modern type was to assume that because the frontal of the skull was missing it did not have a heavy brow ridge and face like Steinheim and Neanderthal. In fact it makes much more sense to assume that it did indeed possess such features. The similarity of the two skulls may indicate that they belonged to closely related populations, which is consistent with the archaeological evidence. They are also linked by the fact that both are thicker-skulled than either typical Neanderthals or neo-sapiens. Indeed far from being the more modern, Swanscombe had the thicker skull of the two and had a slightly less rounded occipital than Steinheim. This very rounded occipital, if it is not simply due to distortion of the Steinheim skull in the ground, is misleading in its resemblance to modern skulls and belies the primitive character of the rest of the skull.

Most of the remaining *Homo sapiens* fossils are thought to be no earlier than the last interglacial, about 100,000 years ago. None are definitely contemporary with Swanscombe, but some could be near. The newest find, from Bilzingsleben in East Germany, is an occipital bone of Holstein interglacial date, provisionally said to resemble *erectus*.

The following pieces may date from about 100,000 to 300,000 years ago: a lower jaw from Montmaurin in the Pyrenees and skull fragments from la Chaise and Fontéchevade in south-west France, Lazaret near Nice and Cova Negra near Valencia. The well-preserved front of a skull from L'Arago cave at Tautavel in the east Pyrenees is perhaps the most significant of these fossils. A complete skull from Petralona in Greece may date from this time; the brain size is 1,220 c.c. Among non-European samples are the frontal bone from Mapa in China and the two skulls from Omo. One Omo skull, like the Solo river skulls from Java, has *erectus* features; the other Omo skull is puzzlingly modern.

Conclusion

Omitting all the qualifications made earlier in the chapter and the tenuous evidence for a robust lineage branching from our own early in hominid history, the pattern of our descent from the apes seems to be as follows. Two to fifteen million years ago our ancestors were small-bodied and small-

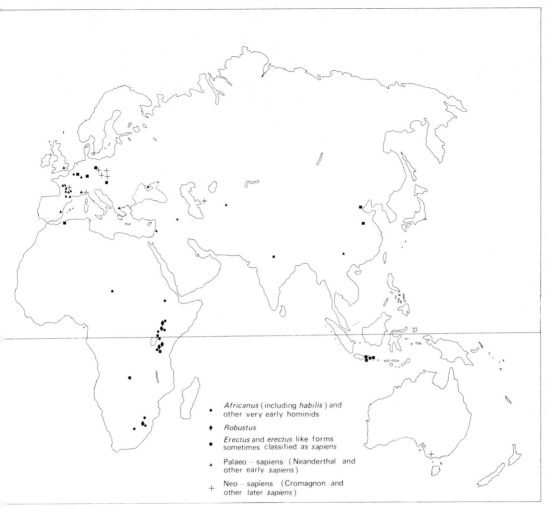

Africanus (including *habilis*) and other very early hominids

Robustus

Erectus and *erectus*-like forms sometimes classified as *sapiens*

Palaeo – sapiens (Neanderthal and other early *sapiens*)

Neo – sapiens (Cromagnon and other later *sapiens*)

Where fossil man has been found.

81

brained but already adapted to walking upright in the grasslands. The hand began for the first time to specialize in precise manipulation and was no longer used in locomotion. The canines were short but the teeth were generally large and were crowded into a relatively short toothrow. Although the body roughly doubled in size, the teeth have continued to get smaller until the present day. Body and brain size came close to our own about half to one million years ago but the modern average brain size was not reached by any fossil men until within the last quarter million years. As recently as fifty thousand years ago, most populations still had the big Neanderthal face and brow ridges, but by twenty thousand years ago they were much like us.

Some physical developments were thus fairly consistent. Body and brain regularly increased in size; teeth became gradually smaller. Other physical characteristics less obviously follow a uniform trend. For example skull thickness increased before a million years ago but then decreased after the time of *erectus*. Brow ridge size seems to have been very variable, larger on average in the *erectus* stage than before or after, and larger again about 50,000 years ago than before or after.

An explanation for these apparent reversals of the evolutionary process probably lies in the operation of two rather complicated processes—neoteny and hypermorphy. The first involves the retention of juvenile features into adult life, the second the premature attainment of adult features. Both are controlled by secretion of hormones from glands. Neoteny, or slowing of growth, can lead to dwarfism or to more slender and child-like features and may account for some of the characteristics of the early hominid, *africanus*, with its small stature and thin bones. It may similarly explain the transition from *erectus* to *sapiens* of Swanscombe type and the later change from Neanderthal to neo-sapiens of modern type. Hypermorphy, or more rapid growth, can lead to giantism and to the heavier brows and bone structure more typical of the old than the young. This may have been the cause of the distinctive body size increase in *erectus* and in some Neanderthals.

Chapter IV The First Men

Man the tool maker

The most popular archaeological definition of man is that he begins with tool-making, and the kind of tools the archaeologist is most likely to find are stone tools. Critics have not been slow to point out that technology in some other substance than stone might have preceded stone tool-making; another school has argued that, since chimpanzees have been observed using tools, either tools are not evidence of human culture or chimpanzees are 'men'.

In the first place there is an important logical distinction between using a natural object as a tool and actually making a tool or artefact; the difference is even more fundamental if the artefact is made with the help of other 'tools' than the bare hands. It has been observed that chimpanzees take twigs or vine stalks and poke into termite hills with them until the termites bite them. The twigs are then withdrawn, and the termites licked off and crunched up. Apparently the twigs are not kept and preparation by breaking them to length or pulling off leaves is rare. In fact this is a classic example of tool-using, as widely found in the animal world. There is no known case of a primate whose tool-using was fundamental to the economics of its way of life. True tool-making is known only in man.

There are similar objections to the suggestion that tool-making was earlier in wood or bone than in stone. For wood to have been made into true artefacts, it would have to be shaped with another tool. What could this be? Until metal knives were introduced very late in human history, cutting tools were almost without exception made from stone. It follows that unless some other substance was available for cutting, wood artefacts could not have preceded stone tools.

The systematic shaping of bone tools by cutting and grinding is a very late development, about 99 per cent of the way through the Stone Age. Previously bone was crudely broken and flaked as though it were stone.

Above *Alternating layers of lake mud and volcanic ash deposited over 2 million years at Olduvai Gorge. Stone tools have been found in the earliest levels. Below left A chimpanzee probing into a termite nest has found a stick to use as a tool. Only man took the momentous step of fashioning his own tools.*

Below *One of the earliest types of stone tool, the so-called chopping tool.*

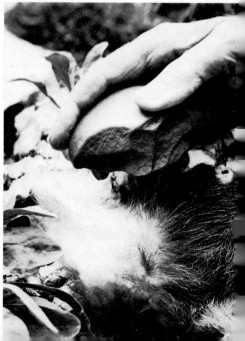

The use of broken bones and toothrows probably goes back to early times, at sites like Makapan Limeworks; but this was little to do with true tool-making.

The earliest stone tools

The flaking of stone tools, while not particularly difficult for humans, would have been a momentous step for an animal to take in a world which had never seen tool-making. It is not impossible that it could have been reinvented many times, and communities could have alternated over the centuries between making and not making tools. But given the advantages gained by the makers of stone tools and the difficulties of inventing from scratch a viable type of stone-flaking, a single invention of stone tools and a continuity of this skill thereafter is much more likely. On such a model, there would be an inevitable time lag in the diffusion of this portentous innovation among early hominids. I suggest that it spread only across the gracile lineage.

The earliest stone tools currently known are from Africa. In the 1930s Leakey showed that there was a whole style of tool-making earlier than the style with handaxes which had constituted de Mortillet's Acheulian or earliest Palaeolithic epoch. In 1951 he named it Oldowan, after Olduvai Gorge where he had discovered it in the lowest bed—Bed I. Meanwhile a claim had been made for similar tools in Uganda, under the name Kafuan. For a variety of reasons the name Kafuan has been dropped. By the 1950s it was possible to show that something rather similar existed in north-west Africa, particularly Morocco, at such sites as Tardiguet and Douar Doum. Here also the evidence supported a pre-Acheulian date.

Estimates of the age of the oldest stone tools have changed a lot recently. In 1951 anyone suggesting that the Oldowan was over a million years old would not have been taken seriously; a 'Middle Pleistocene' date of under half a million years was favoured. Then in about 1961 the newly refined technique of Potassium-Argon dating gave a date of about 1·75 million years for the Oldowan level in Bed I. This result was coolly received and opinion wavered. But soon many other sites with the same early Pleistocene fauna were being dated to this kind of age.

Meanwhile it was concluded on the basis of fossil magnetism in the rocks at Olduvai that the basalt layer on which the stone tools rested could be dated to 1·9 million years. For good measure, Uranium 238 fission track dating was applied and again the date was close to two million years. Soon other east African sites with comparable fauna were being dated within the one to four million year time span, and in hardly ten years serious opposition has vanished.

Surprises continued to come. In the late 1960s at least one stone tool was found in deposits over two million years old in the Omo valley. Then the large scale exploration of East Rudolf began to yield quantities of stone tools. Some seem to be about, or a little over, 2·6 million years old. There are also tools from Kanam near lake Victoria that are expected to be over two million years old.

At the moment there are no tools older than three million years old. Neither Makapan Limeworks, which may be about three million years old, nor the main hominid-bearing levels at Sterkfontein have any stone tools. Of course they might have been adopted later in South Africa. But both the higher levels at Sterkfontein and the Swartkrans site, tentatively in the $1\frac{1}{2}$ to $2\frac{1}{2}$ million year bracket, have stone tools rather like those of Lower Bed II at Olduvai.

Stone artefacts and the products of nature

A problem which obsessed early investigators and still cannot be overlooked is that of distinguishing human workmanship from natural fracturing of stone. Referring to claims that eolithis, roughly chipped stones now widely regarded as natural products, were human artefacts, abbé Breuil said: 'Man made one, God made ten thousand; God help the man who tries to tell them apart!'

It was part of nineteenth century evolutionist thinking that everything evolved from the primitive to the complex. This is quite a useful working hypothesis, which will sometimes be right and sometimes wrong. Gabriel de Mortillet reasoned that if the Neolithic tools were of polished stone and the Palaeolithic tools were shaped by flaking, then there should be earlier tools which were barely modified from the original stone. These were the 'eoliths' of the Eolithic, or Dawn Stone Age.

By 1867 the abbé Bourgeois, not a man whose calling would be expected to bias him towards a Darwinian point of view, was claiming to have found crude stone tools (meeting de Mortillet's specifications for eoliths) at sites of Miocene age in the Cantal region of France. In the 1890s it was Benjamin Harrison, the grocer of Ightham village in Kent, who was finding eoliths, and in the 1920s James Reid Moir and his friends in the Prehistoric Society of East Anglia were searching the crag deposits of Suffolk and Norfolk for traces of Pliocene man. By 1960, all this was very definitely out of fashion. Why?

The present view is that specimens are not accepted as tools if there is any doubt about them being made by man. Secondly they mean little unless they have come from a dated context. Few of the thousands of claimed eoliths were found in geological deposits; they were mostly isolated surface finds. It is current practice to study a collection or assemblage of artefacts found in association before attaching much significance to them. Only subsequently would we be in a position to assess isolated objects resembling them. Eoliths are rarely found in association.

An important theoretical consideration is that the only really convincing reason for developing stone technology in the first place would have been to produce cutting edges. Eoliths are typically devoid of cutting edges, usually being made of naturally split pebbles with irregular and rounded crushing on their edges. Another curious fact is that the small minority of eoliths which came from a proper geological context were from the base of the East Anglian crags; these are marine deposits mostly originally formed fifty metres or more under the sea. Britain at this time was an island, cut off from the continent by high seas, and not a likely place for man to have been living.

Artificial flaking, retouch and tools

Certain principles, which have been established over the last century or so, go a long way towards distinguishing deliberate flaking, by a directed blow, from the various natural causes of stone fracture, such as frost and other thermal action. The way in which flint and other grainless silicate rocks fracture after a blow is called conchoidal. Apparently shock waves radiate out in a conical form (a little reminiscent of a conch shell) from the point of impact and the stone fractures along the plane of these waves. By striking near the edge of a lump of flint, a flake can often be removed; on the face of the flake which comes away from the core there is a swelling adjacent to the point of impact. This bulbar surface has a number of distinctive features.

The flakes removed differ greatly in shape. One variable is whether they were struck off with a hard stone or a softer bone or wood striker or knocked off with a punch. But the most important factor is the initial shaping of the core. This may be quite simply done so that irregular flakes of various

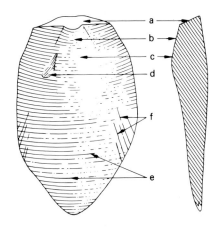

A flake struck by man rather than originating from frost or any other natural agency is recognized from a) the butt, b) the cone of percussion, c) the bulbar swelling, d) the bulbar scar, e) the rings of percussion and f) the striations radiating out from the point of percussion.

Left *Professor François Bordes, a French prehistorian, has learned how to make the main types of stone tool. He can complete the handaxe he is making here in a few minutes.*

Above and right *Stone points hafted by Australian aborigines may reflect Palaeolithic practice.* Below *The Levallois technique by which flakes are removed from a prepared core like this one on the right represents a distinct advance in flintworking.*

sizes come off, or the core may be more skilfully prepared so that the shape of the flakes which come off is to a higher degree predetermined. These will either be blades, long thin flakes so typical of the later Palaeolithic, or they will be prepared core flakes, known to specialists as 'Levallois' flakes; both these prepared core categories are typified by a greater amount of sharp cutting edge round their margin than simple flakes. Towards the end of the Stone Age, blades were made smaller and smaller until some bladelets were under 2 millimetres thick.

The other major way in which artefacts vary is in that the different sorts of 'blanks' can be given different sorts of 'retouch', or secondary chipping. Among many sorts of retouch, a major distinction is between blunting, or backing, in which a blank has its sharp edge blunted with short steep flakes, and a second rather commoner form sometimes called invasive retouch, in which the secondary flaking runs rather further across the surface of the flake.

Backing of one edge sometimes seems to be intended, by blunting it, to prevent the user from cutting himself; more often it appears to be designed to create or strengthen an acute point. Mostly we have no way of knowing why it was done. Invasive retouch varies mainly according to whether it is removed at a shallow angle or a steep one. If it is at a shallow angle, it leaves the edge of the tool sharp, though nothing is sharper than the keen fresh edge of a newly struck unretouched flake. It is possible that retouch was designed to make the edge more durable. Steep retouch can be anything from 45° to 90°; the steeper end of this range can resemble backing and may be for the same function. No flake edge with steep retouch is much

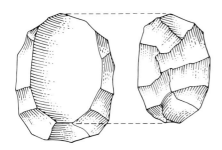 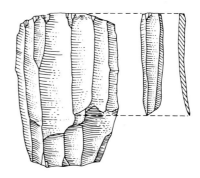

Left *The prepared core technique of flint-flaking. The core of flint (left) has flakes removed from round its edge and from over one surface. The 'Levallois flake' (right) is then removed from this surface of the prepared core by a blow on the faceted platform.*

Right *An advance on the prepared core technique produced the 'blade core' and blades. Manufacture of blades won a considerably greater length of cutting edge from a given core than manufacture of flakes had done.*

use for cutting, but it might be used for planing or scraping. Shallow retouch is sometimes applied by pressure rather than by striking. This brings a level of refinement called pressure flaking which represents the high point of flint-working.

One end product of a century of study of stone tools is a series of names for recurrent shapes that are usually achieved by retouch. The names are either strange, like Levallois points, burins, racloirs and grattoirs, or they are inappropriate, like chopping tools, handaxes and knives. These characteristic types are often referred to by specialists as tools. By now it is a fair bet that the reader is curious to know what they were used for.

Function

The nineteenth century was the great age for speculation among archaeologists on the function of stone tools; books of the time on early man were brim-full of discussions of such topics as whether handaxes were hafted or not. Pioneers like Christy put together most useful comparisons between, for example, eskimo and Palaeolithic tools, and uses were inferred from this. Another Darwinian, Sir John Evans, was still in 1897 discussing the subject; finally he allowed a hint of scepticism to creep into his writing, then despaired of getting any reliable information one way or the other.

Do we know any more today? For example can we now be fairly confident in nominating the functions of the two commonest tools of the first 90 per cent of prehistory, the handaxe and the chopping tool? There are three rather obvious avenues of approach to this problem. We can try to find existing peoples who use tools closely resembling in shape those we are studying. We can look at the tools themselves for visible signs of the wear or damage caused by use, and identify that with specific functions. Thirdly we can examine the context in which the tools are found.

Another type of investigation is sometimes advocated, namely imitation of stone tool-making and experimentation in using them. But there may easily be functions that we have never thought of trying; and the fact that tools can be used in a particular way in modern experiment is no guarantee that they were so used in the past. On the more subtle issue of whether tools had one function or many or none, this technique is powerless.

Ethnographic parallels

There is little doubt that if a chopping tool or handaxe were found in use among a contemporary stone-using hunting society, we would be extremely interested. We would be inclined to generalize this use back into prehistory according to Hutton's principle that the past should, if possible, always be interpreted in terms of the processes and entities that we know today and whose operation we understand. Nevertheless it must be borne in mind that any positive evidence that past usage differed from present usage would immediately override the principle.

As it happens we have no reliable ethnographic data on the survival in use of the main types of early Stone Age tools. For instance the only recorded case of a handaxe in use among modern primitives was among the now extinct Tasmanians, and the tool in question only loosely resembled a handaxe. Though poorly documented, it was apparently an all-purpose tool used, among other things, as an aid to climbing trees, especially by the women; they looped a grass rope round the tree and held that in one hand, while they cut a foothold with the 'handaxe' held in the other hand. This led to the famous story told by William Sollas of how 'a party of lively girls chased by sailors made a sudden and mysterious disappearance; on looking round a number of laughing faces were descried among the branches of the trees into which the girls had swarmed in the twinkling of an eye'! Suffice it to say that this single precise record is hardly a realistic guide to the use of the handaxe.

It is probably worth making a sharp distinction between the use of ethnographic parallels 'on the spot' and their transference to distant and distinct environments, for instance from Australia to Europe. Local parallels probably have a better chance of being relevant. Indeed the men making stone tools today may be the actual descendants of the makers of the tools found by archaeologists. Australia and Siberia are two areas where stone tools were still being made in recent times.

As an example of long distance ethnographic parallels we might take the work of Richard Gould among the Yiwara, stone-using hunters in the western desert of Australia. Tools in use there closely resembled the Quina racloirs (sidescrapers) found for example in south-west France and dating from the Neanderthal period; furthermore they bore signs of the same kind of wear. The Yiwara used them for scraping wood. Was this then their function in Neanderthal Europe? Frankly I do not think so. We know that the Quina occupation coincided with an extreme treeless phase in western Europe's history. At times wood was so rare that mammoth ivory was burnt, and most people have imagined that scraping skins to make skin cloaks was a more likely activity at this time. What are we to do with the ethnographic parallel? This one gives a result that does not fit our other evidence; we must presumably reject it, and accordingly register little confidence in drawing parallels over such distances.

Wear

The evidence of wear may be divided for research purposes into macro-wear, visible with the unaided eye, and micro-wear, tiny scratches and polish visible only under the microscope. Micro-wear is a relatively new study pioneered by Sergei Semenov of Leningrad mainly since 1945. Semenov published a comprehensive treatise on his work containing interesting suggestions on the use of some stone tool types characteristic of the closing stages of the Palaeolithic. The use of the main stone tool types of the earlier Palaeolithic however is not reliably known.

Wear from usage takes the form of chips and scratches, but is it the only cause of such damage on archaeological specimens? Semenov claims that some of the chipping is simply the intended or unintended consequence of the process of manufacture whether the stone was eventually used for anything or not. Secondly, tools found in living areas may have been trampled under foot and damaged before burial beneath the accumulating deposits. Thirdly, some damage may have occurred after burial: frost action is very destructive of stone tools and soil pressure can cause chipping. So even if clear traces of damage are found, it need not have been caused by human usage.

Another point is that if, as it seems at present, some apparent tool types have little wear on them, really serious damage to a specimen is very probably the result of abnormal use or misuse, and will accordingly be misleading. As François Bordes has said, if you habitually use a pen-knife for sharpening pencils, there will be little trace of wear. But if you use it once for cutting wire, this single abnormal act will be indelibly recorded. We may often be left with evidence only for the wrong use of stone tools. If the chopping tool and handaxe were all-purpose tools, attempts to specify a single function (or even a small number of functions) will be misguided.

Functional wear research would be particularly valuable if it made possible the recognition of different patterns of wear on stone tools caused by use on different materials. We would also like to know how much a tool has to be used before wear becomes apparent. Lawrence Keeley has obtained some interesting provisional results by experimenting with his own stone tools on wood, bone, meat and hide. It seems possible that these patterns of wear can be recognized on Palaeolithic artefacts.

Function and context

The last of the obvious avenues for getting at the function of stone tools is the study of the circumstances in which they were abandoned; for in default of a municipal rubbish collection, most primitives leave their tools where they were used.

A tool-kit of handaxes, cleavers and flakes has been found at some sites where we think large animals were butchered. The best examples are two neighbouring sites in central Spain, at Torralba and Ambrona. Working with an international team there, I remember uncovering with my own hands handaxes and cleavers beside the elephant carcases. Similar discoveries have been made at African sites like Olduvai, Isimila and

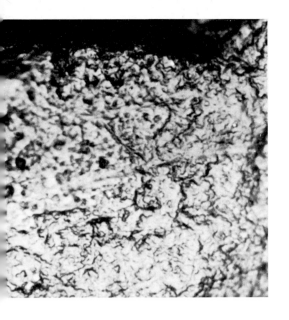 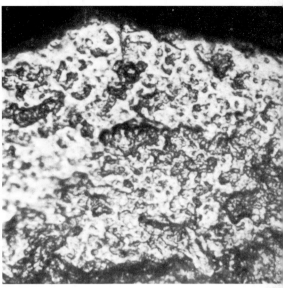

Lawrence Keeley has found by experiment that the worn surfaces of flint tools, when magnified 200 times, can betray their use.

Above left *Scraping bone leaves a polish with a greasy lustre, and shallow striae.*
Above right *Whittling wood leaves a bright and smooth polish; an unworn surface can be seen at the bottom of the picture.*
Below left *Slicing meat erodes the flake scar margins; there are two areas of slight polish.*
Below right *Scraping hide leaves a matt polish and striations.*

Olorgesailie. On the other hand there are plenty of sites of elephant kills without handaxes. Desmond Clark pointed out that there was only one handaxe-like tool at Mwanganda in Malawi, and that sundry flakes, some of them retouched, outnumbered handaxes. There are later sites of mammoth kills in Czechoslovakia where the tools are all small and are mostly bladelets. These cases remind us that there are many different tool-kits which can be used for any one job.

A further example of context belongs to the time of the cave artists. Along the foot of the fine bas-relief carvings in the limestone at le Roc de Sers in south-west France were found numerous, very obviously blunted burins, or flint chisels. There is little doubt that they were used in carving the frieze.

Site context seems to be the principal source of evidence for function. If so, the most commonly voiced reason for studying function will be overturned. Find out what the tools were used for, runs this argument, and then we will know what was going on in archaeological sites. But it now looks as though it will be the other way round; we will know what the tools were used for because we think we know what was being done at the site.

In addition to its site context, each tool or tool type has a more general context which is relevant to its function. If we know something of the diet, economy and environment of a society, certain functions are suggested to us and others ruled out. Probably this kind of reasoning is one of the most sensible approaches to function.

Why study stone tools?
Having discussed at length why we know very little about the functions of individual early stone tools, it hardly needs stressing that their classification into types is not based on function in that sense. Instead it uses our knowledge of the natural categories involved in stone-flaking, such as cores, flakes and retouched pieces. These are then classified into types on the basis of recurrent shapes. Terms such as scraper and knife are unfortunate, just as the blanket term 'tools' is misleading.

The reader could be forgiven for asking why stone tools are studied at all. The answers to this question must be tentative. But the least controversial reason for studying stone tools is that they are the best evidence in the Stone Age for the presence of man in particular places at particular times; irrespective of any knowledge of function, they document man's 'colonization' of the world in the Stone Age. As a consequence we learn about man's adaptation to new environments.

Secondly, all prehistorians accept that in a more or less crude way assemblages of stone tools are characteristic of particular periods. In my opinion they already are, under certain circumstances, a very precise and accurate basis for a time scale for such diverse phenomena as fossil skulls and engraved art objects. All that is required is more systematic and sustained research.

Thirdly, most prehistorians in Europe think that styles of stoneworking, as evidenced in recurrent types of assemblage, identify ethnic groups — people with a common tradition of tool manufacture. Recently there has been much opposition to the idea of distinct culture traditions in prehistoric times, but no hard evidence against it has been offered. To suspend research on the problem at this stage would achieve nothing; I personally believe that the basic idea of defining culture groups according to the stone tools made is sound, and further research will vindicate it.

The human revolution

Recently a revealing point emerged from an analysis of the debris of animal bones at Makapan. Catherine and Dwight Read found that in contrast with normal hunters' accumulations of bones, skulls of bovids were disproportionately common, while the bones of small antelopes, other than their skulls, were absent. Now the skulls are precisely what the carnivores eat last, and the smaller bones of small antelopes are the bits they usually crunch up and destroy. So the Makapan accumulation may be all that an early scavenging hominid could find after the carnivores had sated themselves. Scavenging was possibly the first way in which meat became a significant part of the hominid diet.

In the 1950s John Robinson had argued that the tooth pattern of the gracile hominid *africanus* from Sterkfontein and Makapan was characterized by enlargement of the incisors and canines relative to *robustus* and modern man, while the molars were smaller than those of *robustus*; this seems to be a carnivorous adaptation.

Whereas an animal brought down by man needs butchering, an animal killed by carnivores is already torn open, and a hominid with a taste for raw meat could eat away without a knife. Unless they can be butchered, intact dead animals are not much use as food to a hominid with reduced canines and feeble fingernails. We cannot get at the meat without tools. Stone tools, especially sharp-edged flakes, are the obvious aids. A pointed object, such as a stick cut to a point, is also useful for piercing the animal.

In some localities it is possible to find naturally sharp stones, but early hunters would more often than not have found few effective tools at the place where they had immobilized their quarry. A way of life involving the regular killing and cutting up of animals would be impossible without the ability to make cutting tools, and therefore without stone tool-making. Similarly there is nothing known in primate behaviour prior to meat-eating which makes tools necessary. This is the argument for linking tools and hunting.

95

It once seemed an attractive idea that these began together with the hominid species *africanus*, since his large front teeth were an adaptation to meat-eating. People have even wondered if these factors caused man to break away from the ape line of evolution. But if we take the evidence at its face value, stone tools are known to go back little over $2\frac{1}{2}$ million years. Scavenging and meat-eating at Makapan seem to go back at least three million years and therefore to before tool-making. The large front teeth of *africanus* seem to go back even further, but whether to four, six or even fourteen million years is dubious. It is still possible that we shall eventually find that stone tools are as early as *africanus*, or that both go back to the time of the earliest hominids; but all these seem unlikely at present, and they would make the shortening and blunting of the dagger canines a yet more puzzling phenomenon.

The best idea at the moment seems to be that there were two stages in the switch to meat-eating, some time after hominids first appeared. The first stage sees the development of carnivorist front teeth and scavenging, possibly at the time when *africanus* parts company with *robustus*, conceivably four to seven million years ago. It left him pre-adapted for new advances in carnivorism.

The second stage involves regular hunting and culling helped by tools, with butchery made possible by stone knives that could cut up game not already torn open by predators. This stage will coincide with the first tool-making, and will be the true human revolution. It represents the liberation of man from dependance on other killers, opens up a new range of foods, and gives him greater control over his food supply than ever before.

The origin of language is another of the crucial developments we believe accompanied this human revolution. It is a fascinating and complex problem to which archaeological and fossil evidence can contribute little. During the 1960s emerged a theory that true language differed from the call systems found in other primates in two main ways. Whereas a call system is closed, human language is an open system gaining variety from different combinations. Secondly, true language has the quality of displacement, that is it uses words to represent things and happenings that are not here and now but are elsewhere or in the future or the past.

Charles Hockett suggested that the emergence of true language would coincide with a major behavioural change before the origins of farming. Since it seems to go back well before the time of Neanderthal man, the obvious behavioural advance to equate it with is tool-making. On this model, Hockett's hypothetical human revolution would include speech with tool-making and hunting.

Highly characteristic of human societies is the tendency to monogamy. This too was probably a consequence of the human revolution when an elementary division of labour became convenient between man the hunter and woman the gatherer. It would also increase the chances of survival of

The first men were often monogamous unlike the apes. Surviving hunting communities, including these Bushmen of the Kalahari, perpetuate the early tradition.

the human family unit whose children, with their extended dependency, called for more concerted care and attention after birth than apes ever do.

A suggestion pioneered by Glynn Isaac is that the adoption of home bases characterizes man. He believes that home bases are indicated by what archaeologists call 'living floors'; these are revealed by the careful removal of a usually sterile layer of earth down to what is believed, usually from traces of weathering, to be an old land surface. On this surface may may be found stone tools or food and work debris such as broken bones or edible shells or wood or even excreta. Objects may also have been brought in; they might be stones for weighting down skins or shiny pebbles collected for their attractiveness, or even something brought in accidentally like the tiny marine shells on seaweed used for bedding. Then there are traces of structures: perhaps post-holes or lines of stones.

It needs to be made clear that there is room for doubt on such issues as whether the level is an old land surface, whether objects a few centimetres above it truly belong to it, whether objects on the surface are undisturbed or have been moved by natural forces, or whether an arrangement of stones is an effect of purely natural agencies. Even if all these points are agreed, the interpretation of the surface as a hut or a home base may be controversial.

Two cases of Oldowan sites having possible habitation structures are known. One is near the base of Bed I at Olduvai; it is a semi-circular arrangement of basalt blocks possibly forming a wind-break or hut. Originally it was evidently several blocks high. The other site is Melka Kontoure near Addis Ababa in Ethiopia; here a kind of circular platform was revealed with groups of stones round it. This was two to three metres in diameter while the Olduvai ring was over three metres in diameter.

Man's new territories and new game

The simple tool-making pattern of the Oldowan lasted for a million years or more, but eventually it gave way to a style with handaxes, the beginning of the Acheulian tradition. This seems to have been the work of *Homo sapiens'* immediate predecessor, *Homo erectus*, and falls mainly within the last million years. *Homo erectus* occupied a larger area of the world than any of his predecessors. Indeed it was a more extensive territory than that of any other primate and is exceeded by few animals. Assuming that two million or so years ago man lived only in Africa, from the estimate that he occupied roughly half of its total area, he would have occupied fifteen million square kilometres. I have estimated that when *erectus* colonized Eurasia, he added a further 15 to 20 million square kilometres to his territory. He was in the Far East, India and western Asia. There also seems to have been a sparse occupation of much of southern Europe by this time. This might imply a population of about half a million humans, while the earliest tool makers before *erectus* were probably less numerous, perhaps only a tenth of a million.

Hunting of big game, even of elephants, became normal during the time of *erectus*. One of the earliest examples of this were found, at the same level as an *erectus* skull, in the upper part of Bed II at Olduvai; here were various types of elephant and rhinoceros, and a number of skeletons of *Pelorovis*, a large bovid once thought to be a kind of giant sheep. A date of around a million years is now being suggested for this level. Torralba, too, may date from the end of the *erectus* period and provides evidence for hunting of the largest animals of the region.

There are single carcases of large animals at the base of Bed II at Olduvai and at the top of Bed I. If these are typical kills and if the level they come from is only slightly later than the main hominid level in Bed I, then big game hunting goes back over $1\frac{1}{2}$ million years to the time of *habilis*. On the other hand they may not have been kills at all; perhaps they were found immobilized or dead. There are no big game kills from any of the main occupation levels in Bed I. The biggest animals apparently hunted were antelopes of various sizes. It may be significant that at some Bed I sites frogs, toads, lizards, snakes, birds and small mammals such as rodents, insectivores and bats were very abundant suggesting an emphasis on small game.

cm 0 1 2 3 4 5

This spear, made of yew wood, with one end cut to a point and fire-hardened, was found in pieces among the bones of a last interglacial elephant at Lehringen in Germany.

It is interesting to speculate whether the eventual mastery of the hunting of even the largest animals was due to some technological advance. The larger body and brain size of *erectus* must have helped; after all, a hominid of only 130 centimetres (4′) is at something of a disadvantage against an elephant. I have suggested that the spear may have been invented and diffused at this time; but wooden spears are rarely found by archaeologists, and none are known from African sites; in fact, apart from a dubious example from Torralba, Clacton in England is the earliest site with a spear, and that is only 250 thousand years old.

We would like to know why man spread out of the tropics. Removal of barriers to travel may be important here; the sea level probably dropped considerably during the colder periods of the last million years, establishing land bridges in some places and narrower straits in others. Meanwhile bigger bodies and better hunting abilities would have made the entry into new territories easier. And, according to the Malthusian principle underlying Darwinian evolution, early man's numbers should increase in any territory until the food supply is outrun for only in that way would natural selection take place, but another solution to over-population would be to colonize new land. This would still put selection pressure on the pioneers, a selection perhaps for adaptability since not all of them would be able to cope with the newly presented problems. It is an undoubted fact that man did move into cold latitudes and, in accordance with Bergmann's rule that body size increase is an adaptation to colder climate, the larger body of *erectus* may have simultaneously been encouraged by migration and aided further migration.

Certainly cold winter nights would have been a challenge to man's survival in the middle latitudes, even with a slightly bigger body. Chimpanzees could probably not survive in the open in cool latitudes, and man was probably already hairless, as an adaptation to efficient heat loss when pursuing game. The solution was however at hand in the form of skin cloaks and blankets; and man may also have built shelters. But his most significant invention was fire. We already find traces of it at sites over a quarter of a million years old, notably at Choukoutien in China, Vertesszöllös in Hungary and Torralba in Spain, all supposedly of the late *erectus* period.

Regional diversity

A major consequence of occupying a greater area and meeting a greater variety of environments must have been the pressure to adapt for the first time to different local conditions. Present-day human racial characteristics are believed to be an adaptation to just such local problems. Once a population has adapted to special circumstances, requiring for instance the short limbs and stocky body that aid survival in the cold, replacement would be less likely, a newly arrived population being at a physical disadvantage.

As local physical characteristics began to emerge I suggest that regional cultural patterns developed. After the Oldowan we begin to find that different regions have different kinds of assemblages. In my view two clear regional culture traditions are the Acheulian with handaxes and the Clactonian which lacks handaxes. When the handaxe and non-handaxe assemblages older than about a quarter of a million years ago are plotted on a map they form two distinct provinces. This strongly suggests that we are dealing with culture traditions, and technical characteristics can be listed in both assemblage types which point up the distinction between them.

100

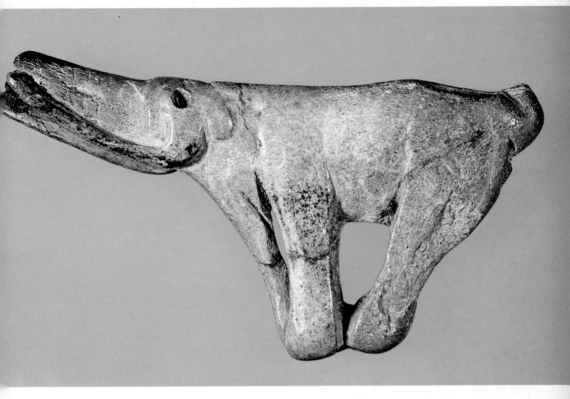

A broken spear thrower from Bruniquel, dating from the end of the Palaeolithic. It takes the form of a mammoth, though the animal has been distorted to fit the shape of the antler it is carved from.

An engraved mammoth at Arcy sur Cure, in one of the northernmost of the decorated caves.

Open air settlement

About the time of the Hoxnian interglacial, a quarter of a million years ago, we start to find considerable evidence for Palaeolithic occupation in western Europe. This is the time of de Mortillet's Lower Palaeolithic Acheulian epoch. It is also Christy's river-drift period, a name which is quite useful because it emphasizes that the tools of the time, our evidence for man's presence, are mainly found at open sites by rivers or, occasionally, by lakes. Accordingly, with other sites of the time rarely found in any other situation, we seem to be dealing with a pattern of settlement with a distinct riverside bias.

This is the time of the richest Acheulian and Clactonian sites like Swanscombe, Clacton (the site after which the Clactonian was named) and St. Acheul (the site after which the Acheulian was named). It is on the basis of assemblages from these sites that we can form a picture of the contrasting culture traditions of the time. A site like Swanscombe reveals Clactonian assemblages buried beneath Acheulian assemblages. There are several different levels with Acheulian, and these suggest a possible evolution. An almost identical evolution has been found further upstream at Yiewsley, just north of London airport.

Cave men

Regular cave-dwelling is well evidenced during the last glaciation, the occupants leaving thousands of artefacts behind, as well as bones and ash and no doubt much organic matter which has decomposed. The debris of human occupation greatly speeds up the natural rate of accumulation of deposits in a cave, conveniently recording, layer by layer, generations of activity. This is true cave occupation and constitutes a special kind of adaptation, a 'cave period', in Christy's terms, as opposed to a river-drift period. Apparently this adaptation did not exist much before 150 thousand years ago.

First perhaps the distinction should be emphasized between, on the one hand, true cave occupation which involved living there, sleeping there, storing food there and leaving the old and young there for protection, and, on the other hand, the business of merely looking in perhaps to shelter from the rain or to have a picnic. It should also be noted that only the entrances of the caves were regularly occupied and most of the sites are simply under an overhang and more correctly called rock shelters or abris.

There are plenty of sites which indicate that men were at least entering caves before a quarter of a million years ago, the time of Swanscombe man. But as evidence of true cave occupation they are all inconclusive. For example two of the earliest traces of occupation in Britain are at a limestone shelter and a cave. A quarry near Westbury-sub-Mendip in Somerset has yielded quantities of animal remains of late Cromer date together with a few undoubted artefacts. Apparently it was formerly a gigantic limestone cavern or overhang in which deposits formed, for traces of stalagmite were found on the floor. But it does not seem to have been very intensively occupied by man.

The other early cave site in England is the famous tourist attraction of Torquay in south Devon, Kent's Cavern. Here we have to rely on nineteenth century excavators' reports, but there seems little doubt that one of the deeper layers contained a late Cromer fauna like Westbury and at least some rough handaxes.

The Sterkfontein caves contained artefacts in the level immediately above that in which most of the hominid fossils had been found, but they were not very numerous and would fit the picnic theory. The Choukoutien fissures may possibly represent an early true cave occupation because they seem to contain a lot of occupation debris; but the evidence is inconclusive because most of it may have been washed in or brought by carnivores. The Vallonnet cave, a few kilometres from Monte Carlo, is at the moment the earliest European site, cave or open, where occupation traces have been excavated. But there are only twelve or so artefacts and no traces of fire with the Cromer-type fauna, and it can hardly be called true cave occupation.

The situation changes considerably when we come to a series of sites of the penultimate glacial or Riss period, where the richness of occupation, and the character of the hearth represent reasonably typical true cave adaptation. They are found in south-west France, south-east France, in Yugoslavia and near Jerusalem. It is debatable whether the cave occupation spans the whole Riss period, or as I suspect, only the later half. For most people the argument whether cave-dwelling began 150 or 190 thousand years ago is somewhat academic. It is an interesting possibility that the fall off in the number and richness of river-drift sites is mainly due to the switch to the cave adaptation.

But there is no question of open sites not being inhabited during the time of cave occupation. In areas where caves were not available, like parts of south Russia or southern Moravia, rich open sites are found. Even areas like the western Dordogne, where caves are abundant, had numerous open air sites during the last glaciation. But, allowing for a bias towards the discovery of cave sites, it seems clear that later Palaeolithic men were seeking out the cave sites preferentially, and this was affecting their pattern of settlement. An example is the way they penetrated to previously undesirable parts of Britain like north Wales, the Creswell limestone cliffs in Derbyshire and the Gower peninsula near Swansea while the previously favoured south-east has little or no trace of their passing.

Two questions are raised. Why was cave-dwelling popular after 150 thousand years ago, and secondly why was it not popular before? The advantages of cave-dwelling are linked with the problems of living in

Europe or Asia north of the 40th parallel during an ice age. A hominid with tropical ancestors is not adapted to being out in the rain and then subjected to cold temperatures. Camping in the open and then being buried in a deep snow fall would have been fatal. Add to this the freezing anticyclonic winds which would blow out from the ice sheet and there would be a high mortality from hypothermia or pneumonia.

Caves and good rock overhangs provide protection from heavy rain and snow. Either naturally or helped by the construction of screens or wind-breaks, they also provide protection from winds and squalls, and stop fires from being blown about or quenched. A south-facing cliff face has remarkable thermal properties. It absorbs solar energy and converts it into warm air for a metre or two in front of the cliff. A true cave also has the extraordinary effect of maintaining a constant temperature in its interior beyond about ten metres from the entrance; it varies a mere four degrees centigrade around the annual mean, while outside the temperature may be plunging to forty degrees below. These are crucial considerations for a hominid whose ancestors had been adapting for millions of years to tropical conditions.

Occupation of caves is not typical of non-human primates and is effectively unknown before the last but one glaciation. Kenneth Oakley has pointed out, in a series of essays on fire and culture, some of the problems which caves present to non-human primates and very early hominids. Apparently they were regularly the lairs of hyaenas and lions. Even supposing one could dispossess the carnivores long enough to settle into the caves, there is the problem of them coming back, especially at night. Monkeys and apes avoid sleeping in caves, and we share with these primate relatives the tendency to snore; the noise of this echoing round the cave mouth would be a fatal invitation to the carnivores to call in for a meal of primate.

These are the probable reasons why caves were not occupied by early hominids before the last but one glaciation. Why was it then at this time that cave occupation began? The answer seems to be bound up with the development of man's control of fire, the ultimate deterrent to predators.

Fire
Fire is in fact found on archaeological sites of some 300 thousand years ago (before the Hoxnian-Holstein), while cave occupation seems to be post-Hoxnian, perhaps 150 thousand years ago. A possible explanation for this disparity lies in the distinction between fire-using and fire-making. The former may involve no more than the utilization of natural fire for a short period. The latter involves much more: the knowledge of an efficient way of making fire; and the possession to hand of the required special fire-making equipment.

Basically there were two ways of making fire prior to the technology of phosphorous and matches; they involve either percussion or friction, and both have been used by hunting peoples. Friction methods resemble the famous boy scout technique of rubbing two sticks together. A simple version, the fire plough, uses a block of wood with a groove or trough in which a second stick is vigorously rubbed; in addition something is needed which will ignite easily from the hot or smouldering wood. Tinder (powdered fungus), wood dust or powdered dry leaves would do. The important point is that all these have to be dry; the right choice of wood also helps.

A superior friction method, which probably came in at the end of the Palaeolithic or later, was the bow-drill. A 'fire twirl', or wooden stick, is rotated in a hollow in a firm timber by looping a bow string round it and running the bow backwards and forwards. The twirl can also be more simply rotated by twisting between the palms of the hands, a technique used by Australian primitives.

The percussion methods usually involve striking a flint against a substance which will give sparks; iron pyrites will do. Again, something like tinder is needed to catch the sparks and ignite some small dry twigs.

All these methods involve considerable forethought and preparation. I suspect that this was beyond the capabilities of the pre-cave dwellers, but came in with, and was helped by, cave-dwelling. The necessary items could be stored in the cave in the dry, and there would be no problem when the fire needed relighting. Of course some contemporary hunters manage to be efficient fire makers as well as nomadic, but this is an advance that probably only came in the late Palaeolithic, and in hostile environments like the far north it involves ingenious and compact fire-lighting kits. Cave-dwelling probably only began with the perfection of a simple fire-making technique.

Fire transformed the way of life of early man. It must have encouraged the closeness of the social group and been useful in making the caves comfortable. The concept of home and hearth are very closely related. Fire allowed the men to dry out after hunting in the rain or snow; previously such expeditions would often have been fatal.

A significant change was probably in food preparation. Careful light cooking releases a great deal of food value not available in uncooked food. Meat can be dried for future use; snow and ice can be melted for water, which would otherwise be unavailable in a glacial winter. Caves, fire and snow facilitate simple refrigeration. Animals killed in the autumn could be butchered and stored in snow heaps or a convenient recess in the cave; but they could not be thawed out without fire.

Left *Fire-making was a relatively late accomplishment of Palaeolithic man. His principal methods would have been friction and percussion. A fire 'twirl' can be vigorously rotated between the palms to generate smouldering heat, by friction, at its base.*

Below *A flint struck with iron pyrites produces a spark by percussion.*

Below *The fire plough was rubbed up and down a groove to make the necessary heat.*

Next page *The interior of the cave of Niaux, where the chambers are unusually spacious. Early cave dwellers probably lived only at the entrances, fearing the dark interiors. However cold it is outside a cave, temperature inside fluctuates only by a few degrees C., a phenomenon which later cave-dwellers may have been able to use to their advantage.*

Cave research

Irrespective of whether they were the normal or exceptional homes of man, caves are a favourable field of study for the archaeologist. They are relatively easy to find, and their deposits are usually well preserved from erosion. Conditions for the preservation of bones are good in the calcium-rich environment of a limestone cave, and it is no coincidence that the earliest complete human skeletons we have were buried in cave deposits.

Caves are outstandingly rich in the number of stone and bone artefacts they contain, and the number of successive archaeological levels in caves like Combe Grenal or Laugerie Haute are quite unparalleled in any open site. Each level is a kind of accumulating living floor, and careful excavation can reveal patterns of hearths or posts from which we might reconstruct living conditions and make certain deductions about the kind of social group in occupation. Our knowledge of the earliest art owes a lot to rock shelters and caves. The thick layers of hearth charcoal are ideal for radiocarbon dating, and there are possibilities of uranium series dating on stalagmite or bones, as well as dating by thermoluminescence and by palaeomagnetic studies on hearths and burnt stones.

A whole science has grown up around the interpretation of cave sediments, taking into account their chemistry, the type, shape and size of the fragments detached from the roof and other details. A broad guideline is that, in milder periods, more humus is incorporated in the deposit, sedimentation is lessened or ceases, and chemical weathering, usually reddening, of the surface begins. In cold wet periods large blocks are liable to tumble from the roof and the overhang may be destroyed. The commonest type of sediment in the Dordogne is made up of small flattish plates of limestone ('éboulis secs'); these are believed to be the product of a cold dry climate. A useful new technique now being applied to cave sediments is pollen analysis.

The near total conservation of bone is particularly valuable. This makes the study of bone tools and deliberate bone-breaking more feasible than in most open sites, where preservation is often poor. Human skeletal material, and especially teeth, are common.

Fossils in the caves have fascinated excavators since Lartet and Christy. Remains of birds, fish and shells, as well as mammals are recovered. They can be analysed to give evidence of the range of animals hunted and of diet, of hunting practices and butchering techniques. They give clues to climate and relative dating.

One particularly interesting line of approach indicates hunting seasons and potential times of the year when the caves might have been occupied. The age in months of younger animals can be determined from their teeth. Since they are all born at the same time of year, which is approximately known, this can be translated into the month when they were killed in the cave. The state of growth of reindeer antlers can indicate the same thing.

Lartet and Christy had already deduced that the caves were occupied for much of the year, and most recent research confirms this. Further research is needed to pinpoint periods of absence, if any, and possible periods when herds migrated through the Dordogne.

A cross check against human preferences affecting the presence or absence of animal remains is provided by owls. Owls tend to roost in caves and drop pellets full of rodent bones into the deposit; the teeth of voles and other rodents, if in sufficient quantities, provide a guide to climate and dating.

It seems likely that cultural evolution took a new turn when cave occupation and a more sedentary way of life became feasible. The focus of innovation shifts from Africa to the middle latitudes and particularly to Europe. The first cave dweller we know much about is Neanderthal man.

Chapter V   Neanderthal Man

Arguably the most fascinating problem in the whole of prehistory is that of the fate of Neanderthal man. Was he the ancestor of modern man or did he become extinct, without descendants? I think the answer may hold the secret to the timing of the emergence not only of neo-sapiens or modern-type man but also of controlled food production and civilization itself.

In common with C. Loring Brace, an American specialist on the Neanderthal problem, I believe it was also the fate of Neanderthal man to have biassed and derogatory biographers. One of the least flattering was Sir Grafton Elliot Smith, whom we have already met in connection with diffusionism. He wrote: 'the large series of skeletal remains that have now been recovered, and in particular the skeleton found in 1908 in a grotto near la Chapelle-aux-Saints by the abbés A. and J. Bouysonnie, affords a clear-cut picture of the uncouth and repellent Neanderthal man. His short thick-set, and coarsely built body was carried in a half-stooping slouch upon short, powerful and half-flexed legs of peculiarly ungraceful form. His thick neck sloped forward from the broad shoulders to support the massive flattened head, which protruded forward, so as to form an unbroken curve of neck and back, in place of the alternation of curves which is one of the graces of the truly erect *Homo sapiens*. The heavy overhanging eye-brow-ridges and retreating forehead, the great coarse face with its large eye-sockets, broad nose and receding chin, combined to complete the picture of unattractiveness, which it is more probable than not was still further emphasized by a shaggy covering of hair over most of the body. The arms were relatively short, and the exceptionally large hands lacked the delicacy and the nicely balanced co-operation of thumb and fingers which is regarded as one of the most distinctive of human characteristics'.

But the man who really sealed Neanderthal man's fate for several decades to come was Marcellin Boule, doyen of French Pleistocene studies, and editor of the influential journal *l'Anthropologie*. Of Neanderthal, he said: 'What a contrast with the men of the succeeding geological

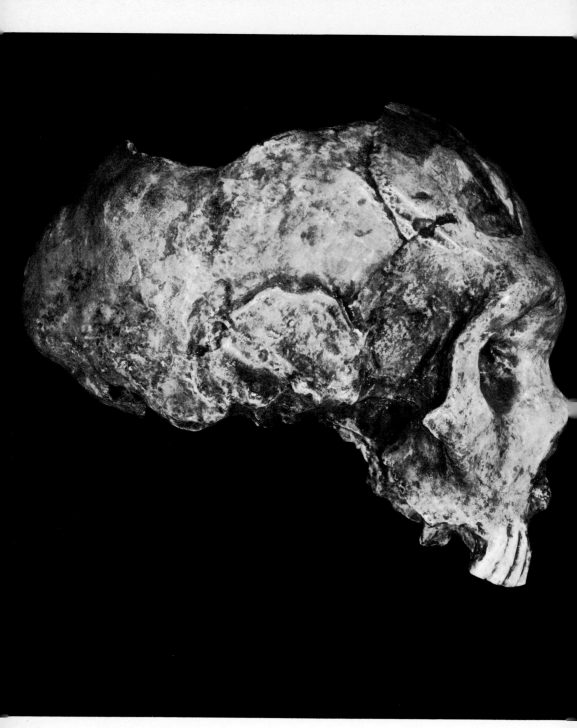

Unrecognized at the time, the Gibraltar skull, salvaged in 1848 during quarrying, was the first Neanderthal found.

period, the men of Cromagnon type, with their elegant body, splendid head, and a forehead high and wide; who have left in the caves they inhabited so many evidences of their skilled handiwork, of fertility of invention, and of their preoccupation with matters artistic and religious, of their faculty for abstract thought; who first merit the glorious title of "*Homo sapiens*"'. Neanderthal man will obviously have an uphill struggle to get back into polite society.

It all started when in 1856 quarrymen blew up the small Feldhof cave in the Neander valley (or Neanderthal) close to Dusseldorf. The valley took its name from the German hymn writer J. Neander, who had chosen to put his original name, Neumann, into Greek: both new and old name meaning new man. Out of the rubble of the blast came a well-preserved skull cap and a few understandably broken bones, but no archaeological finds of any consequence.

German scholars argued about the skull cap. Professor Schaafhausen led the school who thought it was ancient. Rudolf Virchow, one of the most distinguished biologists of the time, maintained that the skull was an anomalous modern one, and that the man had suffered from rickets; the latter observation is probably correct.

In 1864, Neanderthal was discussed at the meeting of the British Association for the Advancement of Science. William King, a professor of anatomy, took the view, as many have done since, that the skull was not the same as the living species of man, and therefore deserved a new name. Accordingly it became *Homo neanderthalensis* King.

At the same meeting, Thomas Henry Huxley, Darwin's most vociferous and successful supporter, who had just published his book *Man's Place in Nature*, took a somewhat different view. The skull was, he said, a bit different from our own, and in so far as it differed it was more like an ape with its large brow ridges and long low skull shape. Such differences perfectly fitted an evolutionary origin for man, still hotly debated at that time. Huxley concluded that the skull probably represented a somewhat earlier stage of our own species.

Huxley had no pre-Neanderthal skulls to compare it with, and effectively only one other fossil differing from ourselves, the Gibraltar skull. By 1908 the situation was very different. Java man was known and Neanderthals were beginning to turn up in quantity.

In March 1908, Otto Hauser, a Swiss dealer in antiquities, was running an excavation at le Moustier. His workmen found a skeleton. With surprising restraint, the full exhumation was delayed some months until invitations had been sent out to a variety of international experts to come and watch the crucial uncovering and removal. Meanwhile, in August of 1908, a second skeleton was found, in the cave of la Chapelle-aux-Saints in the Corrèze department. Both skeletons are now recognized as of Neanderthal type and as deliberate burials.

The le Moustier youth has had a chequered history. Hauser sold the skeleton, over the heads of the French authorities, to the Berlin museum. Two or three attempts were made to reconstruct the skull; all have been much criticized. It was removed by the Russian army in 1944 when Berlin fell. It is damaged, and has still not been adequately studied. The main effect of all this was that the French rushed through an antiquities law to use against future Hausers.

Boule's reconstruction of the man from la Chapelle
The la Chapelle skeleton has had a rather different history. It was quickly transferred to the tender care of Marcellin Boule, who prepared a three volume manograph on it. In the course of his studies, Boule developed a very distinctive view, which soon became widely accepted. *Homo neanderthalensis*, he said, was a side branch of human evolution which became totally extinct at the end of the Mousterian, and contributed none of his physical or cultural heritage to more recent men.

In a much-copied illustration, Boule reconstructed the posture of Neanderthal as though the backbone curved continuously forward and passed into the base of the skull much nearer the back of the head than it does in modern man. A true upright posture requires a backbone which curves back as well as forward to achieve a vertical balance.

Many other ape-like features were detected in the Neanderthal skeleton. The knee joints were supposed to be permanently bent, in a sort of caricature of an old man. He was supposed to have walked on the outer edges of his feet, and his big toe was supposed to have been more mobile and divergent than in modern man. The general impression was of a distinctly ape-like throwback, whom nobody wanted as an ancestor. That the differences were not as great as the unsuspecting reader might imagine could be guessed from the occasional throwaway remarks that these specially ape-like features can be found sometimes in present-day aborigines of Australia and New Caledonia.

In 1957 there appeared an important paper re-examining the question of the posture of the Neanderthal man of la Chapelle. Written by an American anthropologist, William Straus, and an English professor of anatomy, A. J. Cave, it noted how influential Boule's view had been, but that the skeleton itself offered no evidence for his reconstruction. Indeed, previously, a number of experts had expressed reservations, doubting whether such a non-upright posture, with body centre of gravity well in front of the hips, was anatomically possible.

We now know that the doubters were right. Boule was entirely mistaken in his view, and, on the evidence of Straus and Cave, the posture of the Neanderthal or any fossil man was not significantly different from ours.

114

Left *Professor Mikhail Geras-simov of Leningrad made a life-time study and practice of the reconstruction of the facial features of skulls.* Below left *His reconstruction of the features of the young Neanderthal whose skull was found at le Moustier and* (below right) *of the old man, another Neanderthal, found at la Chapelle.*

The main reason for Boule's mistake was the advanced pathological condition of the la Chapelle skeleton. The man in question, perhaps in his forties, had been in poor shape for some time prior to death. The whole spinal column was deformed by arthritis. Interestingly, some other Neanderthal skeletons, like that from Spy in Belgium, used by Boule for comparison, also had arthritis, but less severely so than the man from la Chapelle. The lower jaw was deformed and had lost almost all its teeth some time before death.

Other dubious assertions have been made about the inferiority of Neanderthals. Elliot Smith and Boule both believed that the Neanderthal brain was qualitatively inferior to the modern one. Since Elliot Smith had been able to detect similar stigmata of inferiority in the Piltdown brain case, now known to be modern, some reserve in accepting his conclusions is justified. Clearly they were looking for signs of inferiority and ignoring evidence to the contrary.

The most recent assertion of Neanderthal man's inferiority concerns his speech capabilities. Two American anthropologists, Philip Lieberman and Edmund Crelin, argued in 1971 that reconstruction of the la Chapelle skull reveals strong similarities between the supralaryngeal (or upper throat area) conformation of this skull and of newborn modern humans. Since the latter are incapable of full human speech, it was concluded that Neanderthal man was similarly impeded in his speech.

Whether this assertion is as erroneous as so many other unflattering conclusions, or whether he really was incapable of full speech, is currently being debated. As in previous cases critics are calling for a more widely-based Neanderthal sample to be taken into account, as well as a bigger modern human sample. It is this sort of wider comparison that has eliminated previous errors in our assessment of the Neanderthals.

Arguments for and against Neanderthal extinction
The first of the arguments used by Boule for Neanderthal extinction was archaeological and emerged about 1911 just as the evolutionary assumptions of de Mortillet were being questioned. Sollas suggested that the archaeological sequence in western Europe was not one single continuous evolution. According to Breuil, the makers of the blade tools of the Upper Palaeolithic, which follow Neanderthal man's 'Mousterian' tools in the archaeological record, were invaders from afar. On this view there was no continuity between the two. Therefore the Neanderthals, with their Mousterian culture, died out.

The belief in such invasions had recently become unfashionable. It is now widely held that some of the blade tool cultures of the Upper Palaeolithic develop from the local Mousterian. Indeed it is quite possible that all

116

The Shanidar cave in Iraq, scene of the burial of a number of Neanderthals.

have Mousterian ancestors and that there were ño invasions across Europe at all.

Most of the arguments for the extinction of Neanderthal man use the evidence of fossil skeletons rather than of artefacts and a favourite theme has always been that essentially modern man, sometimes called pre-sapiens, was contemporary with, and living even before, the Neanderthals. This is closely linked with the view that any fossil man significantly different from modern man is disqualified from human ancestry.

The remarkable thing about the theory is how candidates for pre-sapiens vary from one worker to another and from decade to decade. One could cite a long list of now-rejected candidates, from the jaw Boucher de Perthes found in 1863, onwards. Boule, who effectively promoted the pre-sapiens idea, cited Piltdown and two early skeletons from a cave on the Italian Riveria—the 'Grimaldi negroids'. It need hardly be added that the Piltdown fake, being a skull of modern type and age, had no bearing on the problem. And nobody now believes that the Grimaldi skeletons are older than Neanderthal man. Boule had in fact revoked both his candidates by 1923.

In 1932, Louis Leakey weighed in with the Kanam lower jaw fragment and the Kanjera skull bits. But the Kanam piece, with its semblance of a protruding chin, caused apparently by some pathological growth, would no longer be regarded as evidence of pre-sapiens by anyone, while much doubt surrounds the Kanjera bits. Although, like Piltdown, they survived the first application of chemical dating tests as possibly ancient, they have recently been shown by Oakley to be probably much younger than the extinct fauna found near them; there is no longer any convincing reason for considering them very old.

In the 1940s some fragments from Fontéchevade, a cave in the Charente department, were added with Swanscombe to the pre-sapiens list. But few modern workers are satisfied that they are outside the range of the various Neanderthal populations. Today, in spite of the large number of new finds, there is still no good evidence of one or more skulls of entirely modern type to indicate that a neo-sapiens population of modern type lived at the same time as the Neanderthals and that there was an alternative ancestry for modern man while Neanderthal man died out.

There are three more arguments put up against the inclusion of Neanderthal man in our ancestry: no intermediate skulls or skeletons have been found, such as would be expected if Neanderthals had gradually changed into their successors, the Cromagnons of the Upper Palaeolithic (with their resemblance to modern man); there was too little time between Neanderthals and Cromagnons for a transition to have taken place; the late Neanderthals were too specialized to have evolved into Cromagnons.

But I maintain that none of these arguments carries much weight, although the answers to them tend to be somewhat negative because of the

The skull cap found in 1856 in the Feldhof cave at Neanderthal. 'Neanderthal man' has been a subject of controversy ever since.

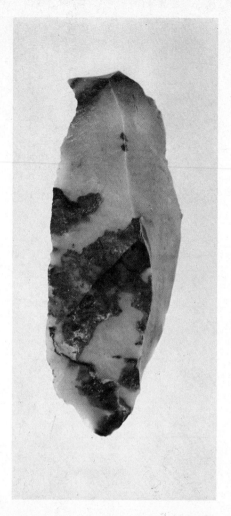

Stone tools can be very beautiful. The 'Levallois flake' on the left is in jet black flint and has remained glossy and unstained. The flake on the right is made of jasper. Both date from Neanderthal times.

incompleteness of our knowledge. We do not, for instance, know with any accuracy the date either of the latest typical Neanderthals, like la Chapelle and la Ferrassie, or of the earliest typical Cromagnons. But the gap may be 30,000 years or more between about 50,000 BC and about 20,000 BC when we have the earliest securely-dated neo-sapiens skeletons in western Europe, like that from abri Pataud. The Cromagnon skeletons themselves are not closely dated but they were poked into the little grotto after the last occupation and are probably post-25,000 BC and possibly contemporary with the majority of French Cromagnon skeletons of 10,000 BC to 15,000 BC. If such a gap really exists in the record of human fossils in western Europe, it would explain why no intermediate forms have been found.

Evidence from western Asia and central Europe may throw more light on a possible transitional period. The Mount Carmel skeletons from caves near Haifa in Israel are so nearly intermediate in form that opinion has wavered between making them Neanderthals or neo-sapiens or a hybrid between the two; at the very least they refute the idea that no skeletons of intermediate form exist. They also seem to be intermediate in date. The skeleton from the Tabun cave, with a radiocarbon date of 38,950 BC, probably dates from the bracket 38,000 to 45,000 BC; some eleven skeletons from the Skhul cave are perhaps five to ten thousand years later, and fall closer to the supposed date of the boundary between Neanderthals and Cromagnons than any other known skeletal sample.

Another series of skeletons of intermediate date and with intermediate features comes from Czechoslovakia. The biggest group comes from Predmost in Moravia, and probably dates from somewhere between 20,000 and 30,000 BC. Some of the males have large brow ridges and robust face and teeth, such as one would expect in the late stages of a transitional population. Possibly a little earlier is a skeleton from Brno, the regional capital of Moravia, and some skull pieces from Zlaty Kun near Prague; these have particularly large brow ridges and other archaic features, and thus also support the idea of a transitional population.

No satisfactory theory has ever been offered to explain what Neanderthals might have specially adapted to, except being Neanderthals. One view discussed below is that they were adapted to a glacial climate, but this clearly does not work for those who lived in warmer climates, nor would it account for the extinction of those in cold latitudes. In summary none of the arguments for their extinction carry much weight.

The compromise view—partial extinction
As late as 1950 it was generally believed that all Neanderthal and Neanderthaloid peoples had died out without issue, but in the last twenty-five years this view itself has met with extinction. Instead, without seriously considering the possibility that Neanderthals in general evolved into neo-sapiens, much of the scientific establishment opted for a compromise,

which divides Neanderthals into two groups within *Homo sapiens*, the classic group (la Chapelle etc.) and the generalized group. On this view the classics became specialized only in western Europe and ultimately became extinct. The generalized group were widespread elsewhere and evolved into modern man.

Anthropologists were impatient to know where modern man came from. They were no longer prepared to accept as our sole ancestors a few fragmentary skulls like Swanscombe and Fontéchevade, from exactly the region where the Neanderthals were most commonly found. Nor was it any longer reasonable to point to vast areas of the world from which fossils were absent, for by this time many of the favoured parts of Asia, like Iran or China, had produced Neanderthals or their assumed archaeological equivalent, the Mousterian. Blank areas were now in short supply.

The compromise theory depends heavily on the Neanderthals falling into two distinct groups. For example the western European classics are all supposed to have a sharp angulation at the back of the skull, but the le Moustier and Gibraltar skulls clearly do not have that feature. On the other hand an Asiatic skull from Shanidar in Iraq is very like some of the la Chapelle group. But recently Brose and Wolpoff analysed a battery of metrical features from the two populations as listed by proponents of the two groups theory to find that, individually, both were very variable and that there was no physical reality to the grouping.

A model proposed by Clark Howell states that the classic Neanderthals, confined to southern and western Europe, were cut off during the first half of the last glaciation and adapted by acquisition of classic Neanderthal features to the glacial environment. Actually, evidence of the distribution of Mousterian occupation in Europe during the last glaciation, and the position of the ice margin, do not suggest isolation. Instead they suggest continuous occupation across Europe with easy access to southern Europe, along the Mediterranean coast.

The idea of glacial adaptation leading to extinction is intriguing, but none of the physical features distinguishing the classic Neanderthals from the Cromagnons (large brow ridges, long low skull or large protruding face) resemble any known cold-adaptation. It is true that the Neanderthals were short and stocky, but then so were some Cromagnons like Chancelade, and several cold-adapted peoples today like the eskimo. It is not a reason for extinction.

One issue relating to cold-adaptation is the reason for the large nasal aperture of Neanderthals. A small and unobtrusive nose would be best adapted to cold climate. But, apparently for anatomical reasons, their very large face, as measured for example by the width between the canine teeth, automatically involves a big nasal aperture. It would be difficult for Neanderthal man in a glacial environment to avoid breathing frozen air on to the lungs and brain base. Coon pointed out in 1962 that the very large

The fourth Neanderthal at Shanidar had been buried with flowers.

nasal sinuses, the canals which bring blood to the nose, were up to seven times as big as those of modern man and may indicate a kind of special air-warming nose, with much more blood in circulation than we have.

The partial extinction theory can be criticized on the following grounds. It postulates the distinctness between two groups of Neanderthals for which there is no satisfactory morphological evidence. It offers no new reasons for believing that European Neanderthals became extinct. It offers no adequate explanation how they could have become extinct and been replaced so quickly by people with an almost identical style of hunting. Above all, it fails to explain how neo-sapiens emerged, because at some earlier stage his ancestors must have had archaic features. It fails to account for the archaeological evidence of continuity in western and southern Europe, and neither the idea of isolation nor that of glacial adaptation is convincing evidence of European Neanderthal extinction.

Neanderthals as ancestors

We must now seriously examine the simple, indeed self-evident, possibility that Cromagnon man evolved from Neanderthal predecessors. The problem is, I think, twofold. Can we find an adequate evolutionary mechanism, an obvious selective advantage in the physical make-up of modern man, to explain his rapid evolution from palaeo-sapiens to the rather different neo-sapiens form? Is there an adequate reason why this should have happened about thirty to forty thousand years ago, bearing in mind that, if they had been previously selectively advantageous, these changes should have set in much earlier?

Loring Brace argued that large front teeth are a key to the physical change from palaeo- to neo-sapiens. He argued that the Neanderthal hunters' diet required larger front teeth than later people had and the lower face in which they are set had to be bigger and stronger. The brow ridge helped to anchor the muscles involved, and the protruding back of the skull counterbalanced the big face.

Brace suggested that, at the close of the Mousterian, eating and cooking habits may have changed. The better cooked food needed much less tearing and mastication, and the teeth and their facial setting could reduce rapidly in size. The theory is intriguing. However, a great many separate mutations would be necessary to produce smaller front teeth, smaller face, taller forehead and other skull shape changes; it seems a little implausible that this could all happen in twenty to thirty thousand years without a very strong selective pressure. Archaeological evidence at the moment offers no support for the view that cooking or eating habits changed at this time.

A second explanation of the way Neanderthal man might have evolved into modern man owes much to Sir Gavin de Beer, former director

Left *The skull of the Neanderthal boy from Teshik Tash cave in the Himalayas.*
Right *Gerassimov's version of the facial features of the Teshik Tash boy.*

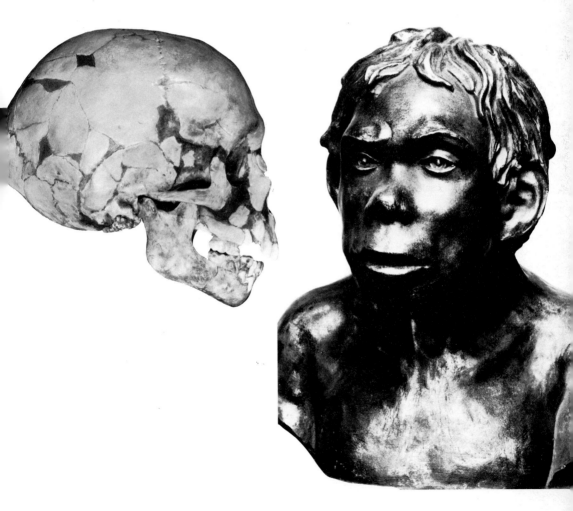

of the Natural History Museum and eminent evolutionist. I have added a number of elements to it. Two major clues support this theory of the origin of neo-sapiens and his relation to palaeo-sapiens and earlier hominids. Firstly, a number of infant Neanderthal and pre-Neanderthal skulls have been found (Staroselje in the Crimea; Pech de l'Azé in the Dordogne; Modjokerto, a juvenile Java man; and Taung, the juvenile gracile hominid). They all more closely resemble modern man than do adult fossil hominids. The same is true of juvenile apes. In fact, Staroselje has all the characteristics of skull shape, lack of brow ridges, small face and so on, which distinguish neo-sapiens from palaeo-sapiens. Cromagnon skulls resemble juvenile Neanderthals. Why?

The second clue was forcibly brought home to Sir Arthur Keith, eminent anatomist, in the 1930s. A skull found at Gardar in Greenland was the subject of controversy. Although it was from a Norse settlement of the twelfth century AD, it resembled Neanderthal skulls, and had been dubbed *Homo gardarensis*. The matter was resolved when Keith examined a collection of pathological skulls in the Royal College of Surgeons. The Gardar skull was easily matched by several which were the result of a strange malady called acromegaly.

Acromegaly results from irregularities of the pituitary gland whereby the whole balance of hormone secretion and thus of growth pattern is altered. The evolutionary equivalent is hypermorphy, discussed in chapter III, which can produce acromegalic features or giantism. The more extreme Neanderthals may well be the result of hypermorphy, which is known to be an adaptation to cold. The opposite of hypermorphy is neoteny which has the effect of slowing growth and results in the retention of juvenile features into adulthood. The difference between juveniles, with round skulls, smooth bulbous foreheads and small faces, and old men, with sloping foreheads, big brow ridges and a generally hairy and aged appearance, is a microcosm of the whole duality and balance between neoteny and hypermorphy.

Neoteny and evolution

In his standard work, *Embryos and Ancestors*, de Beer explained the important role of neoteny and hypermorphy in evolution. It is full of oblique hints that man's present physical form is due to neoteny (retention of juvenile features).

The details are never spelled out but there is no real doubt that neoteny occurs, and though it is strangely rarely mentioned in connection with Neanderthal man, evolutionary textbooks like those of J. Maynard Smith, J. Z. Young and T. Dobzhansky accept that it has definitely occurred in human evolution. An analogous phenomenon is actually found in a living animal, a salamander called the axolotl; this can develop into a

126

normal salamander, or became sexually mature while still in the larval stage, apparently for environmental reasons. The fact that an animal can be genetically constituted so that it has the alternative, shows how feasible an evolutionary genetic change from one to the other would be.

There is good evidence that the growth process in man takes roughly twice as long as in the African apes, while foetal duration and onset of sexual maturity are little delayed: foetal period in humans 9 months, in apes 8–9 months; onset of female fertility in humans 11–13 years, in apes 9 years. The neoteny, or more prolonged growth, of humans is indicated not only by such things as the dependancy period, several years after birth of helplessness unique to humans, but to much hard quantitative data: commencement of milk tooth eruption in humans after 6–8 months, in apes after 3–4 months; permanent teeth eruption in humans at 6 years, in apes at 3 years; finally, duration of growth after birth in humans 20 years, in apes 10–11 years.

There are so many features in adult humans which are matched only in the juvenile stage of apes that it is almost a game to collect them. The form of the *labia minora*, or skin flaps beside the vaginal entrance, is similar in juvenile apes and humans; the ethmoid and sphenoid bones of the skull are separated by a thin extension of the frontal bone in these two, but not in adult apes.

Neoteny may have occurred several times in human evolution. For example the earliest hominid branching off from the common ancestor may have been neotenous, some of the more gracile forms of *africanus*, and the early *sapiens* population represented by Steinheim and Swanscombe may have been similarly altered. By the same token hypermorphy was probably responsible for the emergence of the *robustus* type, the big bodied and thick skulled *erectus* type, and the big classic Neanderthals.

Among the advantages of neoteny are the more bulbous frontal lobe, where a lot of brain work seems to go on, and the longer potential learning period that it must bring. The brow ridges would have become redundant when the frontal lobe became bulbous and the forehead over-hung and protected the eyes. What we need is an explanation why neoteny should have been operative about thirty-five thousand years ago.

Neanderthal brains and childbirth

Probably the most extraordinary fact about the late Neanderthals is their large brain size; it was actually larger than today's average. The skull from Shanidar dating from about fifty thousand years BC had a 1,700 c.c. brain. A small group from western Europe of similar age, and associated with a single culture, the late Charentian, were similarly enormous: la Chapelle 1,600; la Ferrassie 1,641; Circeo 1,550; Spy I 1,525; Spy II 1,425 and la Quina 1,350. The last two were female. The males average close to 1,600 c.c. Since the last interglacial they seem to have increased by over twenty per cent, and they were some fifteen per cent bigger than today's average.

Other things being equal, large brain size would seem to be an adaptive advantage, but evidently it is not as simple as that. The relative size of different parts of the brain seems also important, and neoteny offered an improvement here, even though it would tend to decrease the overall size. Genes for a bigger brain must be available all the time. But there is a very good reason why it does not go on increasing to well over 2,000 c.c.: it is the problem of child birth.

Every child born normally (without Caesarian section) has to pass, usually head first, through its mother's pelvic aperture. There is very little room to spare. In fact the child's head has to be forced through, and is usually somewhat deformed in the process. This squashing of the skull is only possible because the skull bones are poorly fused, joined by cartilaginous strips which ossify later; in the apes they become rigid at a much earlier stage. Imagine the predicament of Neanderthal mothers, whose pelvic size was much the same as in the last interglacial or today, trying to give birth to babies whose brain size had increased by twenty per cent, and whose skulls were probably too rigid to squash. Infant mortality normally running in non-literate hunters at about fifty per cent would rise steeply to ninety per cent or more.

The perfect escape mechanism, with numerous linked advantages, was available to release them from their impasse; probably the necessary genes already existed in the population. In apes, and no doubt in the common ancestor, the child's brain size is at birth fifty-five per cent of its full size; in modern humans it is only twenty-three per cent of full size. This is the new lease of birth, which neoteny has given the big-brained. I suggest most of it came at the end of the Neanderthal period as a result of the outstanding selective pressures operating at childbirth; those infants with a relatively low birth-to-adult brain size percentage would have become the parents of the next generation.

All kinds of other selective advantages of neoteny may be suggested, but it is unclear how important they were. Sexual selection may have done a lot to eliminate, as sex partners, women who retained strongly Neanderthal features and may have favoured those with child-like, neotenous features. It has been claimed that acromegalics are more gentle than other people; if this were true it may have hastened the decline of the Neanderthal genetic type in an increasingly aggressive population.

There are many racial features which are known to be neotenous. The Bushmen possess some of them, such as thin hair on the head; the Mongoloids have others. Europeans have light skin—an undoubted neotenous feature. This may have been particularly advantageous in Europe, the most sunless quarter of the world, for rickets seems to have been common among Neanderthals and two preventatives are to synthesize more vitamin D from sunlight through a lighter coloured skin or to eat more vitamin D in the form of fish. Our ancestors probably did both.

In summary, none of the arguments for believing that Neanderthal man was incapable of evolving into ourselves carry much conviction. The more natural view is that he was our ancestor and that the mechanism was neoteny. It has benefited us in many ways, but the fact that it would have greatly multiplied the number of surviving children at the end of Neanderthal times seems to be the most likely explanation why we became what we did when we did; and why, child-like, we have invented an accelerating technological economy and have a consuming love of the arts and other forms of play.

The first glimmerings of higher culture

The first signs of art and symbolism may be seen as heralding the dawn of higher culture. In view of the controversy discussed above, it is interesting to note that the kinds of phenomena which one would expect to lead us to true art first occur in the Neanderthal Mousterian.

True art, in the form of representations of animals in painting and engraving, first appears a little before 30,000 BC at sites in the Dordogne. There is no reason to believe it is earlier, or even as early anywhere else, but it is similar in date in central and eastern Europe. An essential prerequisite was the ability to cut stone or bone and to find pigments for painting. Both these skills are demonstrated at an early date in the Mousterian. Surprisingly the carving consists of unmistakable symbolism.

The collection of pigments, both iron oxide and manganese dioxide, is documented in a number of Mousterian sites. One explanation is that body painting was widely practised in this culture; we have no hint of any representational art.

The carving of extremely simple symbols is also found. A pebble from Tata in Hungary has a cross engraved on it. A rough limestone block serving as a tombstone for a six year old child's grave at la Ferrassie has a series of carved hollows over it, and one larger hollow, or cup mark. In later chapters we shall be looking at cult evidence as diverse as cave bear trophies, grave goods, pyramids of stones and clay balls flattened against the walls. But there is no doubt that the first groping steps towards painting and engraving belong to the Neanderthal period.

Chapter VI   The Cave Artists

The great flowering of cave art dates from the later and possibly colder half of the last glacial period, the archaeologists' Upper Palaeolithic, spanning twenty-five thousand years between thirty-five and ten thousand years ago. Apart from a possible extension into Siberia, the cave artists are known only in Europe at present.

The distribution of decorated caves

Well over a hundred decorated caves are known in France and Spain. They vary from the well-known and spectacular like Lascaux, to the extremely minor like Gouy, a small cave in the chalk close to Rouen (Seine Maritime) with some rather featureless engravings. New caves continue to be discovered, and it may be predicted that more remain.

There are three particularly important concentrations: the Périgord, the Pyrenees and Cantabrian Spain, the last two areas being almost continuous. The Périgord is the region of cretaceous limestone taking in the Dordogne department and part of the Charente. The strip runs diagonally from near the coast around Cognac in the north-west, down to near Gourdon (Lot) in the south-east.

The Périgord is outstandingly picturesque, with its limestone gorges and cliffs, its wooded hillsides and its ancient villages and castles. The Palaeolithic sites cluster round Les Eyzies and the Vézère valley, where Lartet and Christy first concentrated their efforts. In this valley are Lascaux, Font de Gaume and Combarelles, as well as a host of less well-known sites.

Niaux, not far south of Foix (Ariège), is amongst the three most spectacular painted caves. The complicated cave systems of Tuc d'Audoubert and les Trois Frères are situated one over another in the same department. A fourth long system is at Montespan (Haute Garonne). At the west

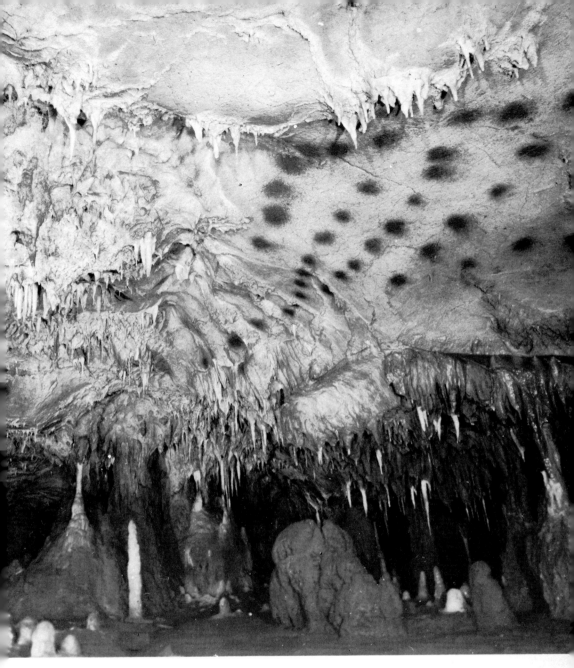

Rows of blobs of paint decorate the cave at Pech Merle.

end of the Pyrenees are some caves with exotic Basque names like Etche-berriko-Karbia (Basses Pyrénées). While only a few caves in the Périgord are as long and complex as for example Rouffignac in the Dordogne which has some eight kilometres of galleries, many Pyrenean caves are extensive and tortuous or contain underground rivers. Montespan is quite dangerous, while Niaux is easy enough to walk through but its paintings are ranged through spacious galleries often over a kilometre from the entrance. The Pyrenean 'karstic' cavern systems have formed in a narrow strip of lime-stone surrounding the high Pyrenees. The slopes are much steeper than in the Périgord, and the hills are higher.

Without much of a break, the caves and limestones of the Pyrenees continue along the north coast of Spain through the Basque country to the Cretaceous limestone of Santander and even beyond into Asturias. This is the Cantabrian province, and Altamira, in its centre, is often regarded as the premier painted cave—'the Sistine chapel of prehistory'. The conical hill of Monte Castillo has four painted caves in it and evidence for a long sequence of occupation. One of the most recent discoveries is the Tito Bustillo cave at Ribadesella near Oviedo; the whole area is rich in painted caves and more will surely be found.

The distribution of painted caves continues across the varied environ-ments of Iberia, to Escoural in Portugal, the westernmost cave. There are several decorated caves in Andalucia, and these are the southernmost and nearest to Africa. Mediterranean Spain has few Palaeolithic decorated caves; instead it witnesses the fascinating 'Spanish Levant Art', whose age is probably post-Palaeolithic.

Between the Pyrenees and the Périgord, in the region called Quercy, there are more sites, notably Pech Merle (Lot), one of the most important, and a new site close by at Pergouset. Sites extend northwards into central France, where Angles-sur-l'Anglin (Vienne) and Arcy are among the most important. There is a small group in the Rhône valley but, otherwise, eastern France and points further east are without painted caves. In central Italy there is a single painted cave, Paglicci, which is on the Adriatic side; there is a series of engraved caves of high quality but very late Palaeolithic date in southern Italy and Sicily. Further east the only well authenticated art is found in Kapovo cave in the Urals.

In *The Art of Prehistoric Man in Western Europe*, André Leroi-Gourhan has given some useful data on the depth inside the caves that prehistoric painting and engraving is to be found. He lists 27 occurrences in the entrance or daylight zone; 30 occurrences lie inside the cave but are of easy access (less than 50 metres); 5, though near the entrance, are difficult to reach; while 15 are deep inside the cave. It must be understood that we are rarely sure where the original entrance was, and sometimes simply do not know. Nevertheless it is fairly clear that the majority of art is neither near the entrance to the caves nor very far in, while enough examples are known of deeper positions to indicate that, on occasion, men penetrated deep inside caves to paint. Work at the entrances to the caves falls into two groups: one of bas relief carving and another, older series, of simple engravings, possibly dating from before man dared to go regularly into the caves.

Techniques of carving and engraving

Pictures in the caves involved two basic techniques, painting and carving. The most ambitious and laborious projects must have been the bas reliefs, which were carved in limestone, a mercifully soft rock. They are generally covered by occupational debris which enables us to date them. The earliest, from Laussel (Dordogne), includes the famous 'lady with the cornucopia' and a series of other blocks, mainly with female figures on them, must date from about 20,000 to 25,000 BC. A very low relief on the ceiling of the tiny cave called abri du Poisson in the Gorge d'Enfer of Les Eyzies was sealed from access about the same time; it depicts a fish of the salmon family. Most of the bas reliefs belong to the Solutrian or Magdalenian periods after 20,000 BC.

The two most remarkable Solutrian friezes are from Roc de Sers (Charente) and Fourneau du Diable near Bourdeilles (Dordogne). At least ten animal figures are included in a great row of blocks aligned for several metres along the cliff wall at Roc de Sers while just two very distinctive wild oxen, with an indistinct third, make up the frieze at 'the devil's furnace'. At the foot of the Roc de Sers frieze, archaeologists found a large number of blunted flint burins. Evidently a good many had been used in carving the bas reliefs.

Two exceptional Magdalenian friezes are known. One is at the northerly site of Angles-sur-l'Anglin and includes three female figures and some animals. The other is at Cap Blanc near Les Eyzies. The latter consists mainly of horses, though there are traces of a bison. The horses are not merely very beautifully modelled by the carver, they are also very large by Palaeolithic standards, one being two metres (6′) long. They are slightly damaged and no doubt they only survived because they were buried by the accumulating occupation deposit.

Except for the horse head from Commarque, close to Cap Blanc and Laussel, carved in very low relief some way inside a cave, bas reliefs are not found far into the caves. No doubt this is because the amount of time and light needed to finish them was much greater than for a painting. Even the painting must have stretched their resources for the men of the time had only primitive stone lamps.

Distantly related to the limestone relief carving are a number of cases of modelling in clay. Probably the best are the bison of Tuc d'Audoubert, modelled slightly flattened against the cave floor. Unfortunately, with slight

Above *A bison from Tuc d'Audoubert in the Pyrenees has been modelled in clay.*

Below *A fish of the salmon family is sculpted in low relief in the roof of a little cave near Les Eyzies.*

134

changes in the environment of the cave, they show signs of cracking up and we will perhaps never know the full extent of what may have been a common art form in prehistoric times if its examples have always been subject to such rapid disintegration.

By far the commonest form of surviving cave art is line engraving. It has a great deal in common with painting: it depicts almost exactly the same kinds of subjects; the prevailing style of outlining with occasional restrained shading is shared.

Engravings are found from Sicily to Normandy and from Spain to eastern Europe. In the later stages of the evolution of engraving we suspect that eventually it was almost always done with a burin. At the very dawn of cave art, burins were not yet common; the 'reindeer' from Belcayre (Dordogne), probably carved a little before 30,000 BC, seems to have been roughly hacked or pecked out with a pointed pick-like object; only the head shows traces of a finer engraving tool. By about 27,000 BC the finer technique, no doubt due to the practised use of the burin, is found at sites like la Ferrassie. Incidentally the pecking technique has been widely used in more recent times in other spheres, as in Saharan rock art, and in the Bronze Age engravings of Val Camonica in north Italy.

Techniques of painting

Painting in Palaeolithic Europe was technically very simple. Only two mineral pigments were used: iron oxide, mainly in the form of limonite or haematite, and manganese dioxide, a black pigment; carbon has never been found used in this context. Primitive artists in other continents have usually used at least one other colour; white paint for example was common in Australia, and was used in prehistoric African art. Because limonite varies in colour from yellow through red to dark brown, and because manganese is often purplish, an effect of multiple colours is sometimes obtained, notably in the case of the so-called polychrome painting of Font de Gaume and Altamira.

Both limonite and manganese were available to the cave artists, for they occur in the limestone the caves have formed in, and can be picked up today. Lumps were used as crayons in Mousterian times; examples from Pech de l'Azé still have bevelled ends from use. Later the paint was obviously powdered, sometimes being strewn about, over burials for example. A small flat limestone plate was found in the archaeological deposits at Arcy sur Cure (Yonne); it had clearly been used for carrying ochre, and still had a little piled on it. A bone tube from the site of les Cottes (Vienne) had evidently contained powdered red pigment. Whether the powdered paint was mixed up into a paste or a liquid is not known.

As to the method of applying the paint to the walls, we have few clues.

Above *At Pech Merle, paint was probably blown on through a tube to outline the hands.*

Below left *The stomach and hump of this bison at Niaux are shaded, a normal practice in late cave art.*

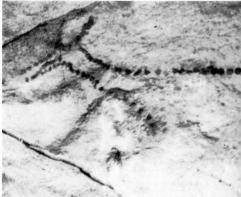

Above *Deer on the walls of the cave at Covalanas in northern Spain are outlined by paint applied with the finger tips.*

A bison at Font de Gaume, one of the few caves where the paintings have been successfully cleaned since their discovery.

Engraving of a bison and a horse in the small Dordogne cave of Gabillou. Some of the most exquisite of all engravings have come from this little-known cave.

Some probably early painting such as that on the walls of the Covalanas cave in Santander had apparently been carried out with the finger tips, and is little more than a line of finger blobs. Elsewhere the finger blobs had been run together by smearing.

In the case of the well-known hand silhouettes, which find later counterparts as far afield as Australia and New Guinea, the paint has been blown on. This could be done quite easily through a short bone tube, the paint being blown from the mouth. The Pech Merle hand silhouettes surround a pair of horses which have blobs all over their bodies. The blobs were probably blown on through the same tube, and even the outline of the horses seems to have been sprayed on in this way.

A bone tube found in France at an early Upper Palaeolithic site had contained powdered red ochre and was obviously an artist's paint tube.

There are a number of examples of painting, especially where two or more colours are employed, in which the colour shades off in a delicate and subtle way. Examples are found at Font de Gaume, Altamira and Lascaux. That some sort of brush was being used seems highly likely, though a fur pad might also achieve this effect.

The technique of representation consists above all of outlining the animals. In the later stages, subtle shading of the stomach or neck was common. The head was sometimes 'blocked in'. But examples of the whole animal being blocked in in a single uniform colour are virtually unknown, though this kind of silhouetting is common in primitive art, and practically universal in the distinctive Spanish Levant style. A couple of little horses from Lascaux are almost blocked in, but lack sharp silhouetted edges. Where several shades were used in the later polychrome painting, it was not unknown for the whole animal to be filled in.

Subject matter

The entire range of subjects of both painted and engraved cave art falls into two main categories: the animal and the symbol; a third category, the human figure, is rare and usually stylized.

In the case of the animals, the primary objective always seems to have been to show the most easily recognizable view, namely the lateral outline. This often presented problems in depicting the horns or antlers. One solution was to show those too as though seen nevertheless from the front, in the manner called twisted perspective. A variety of more or less satisfactory visual compromises was tried but true perspective, in the modern or renaissance sense, was never employed.

Perhaps the limited range of subject matter can be underscored by listing all the things which might have been included but were in fact omitted. There is no horizon or sky line, no trace of trees, plants or other topographical features, no sun or moon or clouds. Furthermore there were no scenes in our sense of the concept. Maybe there were compositions in the sense of deliberate juxtapositions, but no scenes show several animals on the same level and drawn at the same size; none associate them with humans drawn to scale and realistically taking part in the proceedings; there is no explicit case of an animal in action.

Siegfried Giedion, the Swiss art historian, has pointed out that there is not even a systematic commitment to the horizontal axis, so typical of western art. Pictures occur at all angles to one another and to the ground. They occur at all scales, and often one on top of another. This last feature, called superposition, has led to some varied interpretations. At first abbé Breuil, doyen of cave-art studies from 1901 until his death in 1961, thought it was primarily a guide to whether the paintings were early or late in the cycle. Latterly, André Leroi-Gourhan has suggested that it indicated association between the animals. It may also betray a feature very common in primitive art, namely transparency. This is the idea that the internal organs of an animal, or whatever is behind it, should be included in the picture, as if they were in no way obscured.

The symbols may be divided into those which are obviously representational, mainly the vulvar symbols and penises, and the remainder, which are somewhat more enigmatic and disputed. Some of these latter are very simple, and might be disregarded as doodles: for example rows of discs or blobs and rows of lines. Others are much more complex, and often so large and impressive that Giedion has called them the 'Great Symbols'. With few exceptions they are rectilinear and compartmental. Division into three parts is specially common.

Leroi-Gourhan divides them differently: into wide symbols, such as the 'tectiforms' and 'scutiforms', and narrow symbols, such as 'claviforms' and 'penniforms' and other linear shapes. He goes on to make the not unreasonable suggestion that the narrow forms are male, or penis-like, while the wide ones are female, derived from vulvae. In my view the genuine symbols of male and female sex organs are so explicit, as we shall see below, that it is probably a mistake to interpret less explicit symbols in this way, unless their stylization can be clearly followed. For Giedion, all the great symbols are deliberately obscure, and were meant to be incomprehensible to all but initiates; as far as we know, no clue was left to their interpretation.

Above *A fine horse in the axial gallery at Lascaux where several colours have been used but the body is nevertheless not completely painted in.* Below *Squared signs like this 'tectiform' at Lascaux (top right) are common in cave art but their significance remains a mystery.*

Humans are rarely portrayed in cave-wall art, but more commonly appear in small objects, such as statuettes, decorated tools or plaques. Some of the best-known humans in wall art are the 'speared men' of Cougnac and Pech Merle; there are also the men with animal heads which are discussed below.

Altamira

It is a strange fact that when the well-meaning but naïve Don Marcelino de Sautuola, gentleman and landowner in the area where the cave of Altamira lies, announced his discovery of paintings there in 1879, his claim was met with almost universal rejection. Contemporary experts, admittedly in a period when expertise was at a low ebb between Darwinian enthusiasm and the renewed burst of research which began with the new century, were very quick to find reasons for dismissing it. The story soon got around that de Sautuola had an artist staying with him who had obviously faked the pictures. It is all the more strange because Lartet and Christy had recognized a number of exquisitely fine carvings in antler and ivory which had been accepted as genuine without serious question.

De Sautuola had apparently been exploring the cave for some time, since a dog had fallen into its narrow entrance. The story goes that his young daughter, Maria, wandered into the first low gallery on the left of the passage while de Sautuola was digging in the entrance. The gallery is so low that when I visited it in 1959 it was still impossible to stand up inside it and it was therefore very hard to see the paintings on the ceiling; the floor has since been lowered. Young Maria had no such problems and excitedly informed her father: 'Toros, toros'—'there are bulls here'. She had discovered the ceiling with paintings of extinct bison.

Between 1895 and 1900 more decorated caves were found, mostly in France. A point was reached where the truth could no longer be denied. Emile Cartailhac, the main opponent of authenticity, sent the young abbé Breuil to see if there was any reason to doubt these discoveries. When it was clear they were genuine, Cartailhac magnanimously apologized for his part in opposing them. Cynics have said that, if Altamira had been in France, the French dominated establishment of early prehistory would have hailed the 'Sistine chapel of prehistory' immediately. Instead they had to wait until 1940, when 'the Louvre of prehistory' was discovered—Lascaux.

Lascaux

1940, actually the year when three decorated caves were found in France, was an unfortunate year for Lascaux to be discovered, and it has been dogged by odd luck ever since. Hitler's Germany had just taken the country over and imposed a military occupation in the north. Apparently four boys,

Ravidat, Marsal, Agnel and Coencas, found the cave and reported it to the local schoolmaster, who in turn called in abbé Breuil. There is a persistent story that a dog fell into the cave, and it is repeated in many popular books. The dog even has a name—Robot. But the principals have since denied that any dog was involved. No doubt there was a confusion with the Altamira story. Evidently no good tale of the discovery of a cave is complete without a dog, preferably both a dog and a child.

For the duration of the war little information was available on Lascaux. Indeed English prehistorians did not even hear of it. Some photographs appeared in a journal called *Illustration du Midi*. Amongst these was a scene which has since become famous: this is the shaggy bison with a spear through him, and lying diagonally beside him the unprepossessing little man with a bird head and a large erect penis. But the first photograph of this scene showed only the tiniest traces of a penis on this celebrated gentleman.

Years later some misguided opponents of cave art pointed out that the penis had become much larger in the original than in the photograph; it was obvious, they said, that the whole thing was fraudulent, and someone was adding to it. The truth is more bizarre still. The editors of the war-time magazine, chosen by the Vichy government for their prudery and cooperation, had thought fit to paint out most of the penis, lest it should shock.

In a somewhat similar case, André Breton, the surrealist, had visited Pech Merle where one of his political opponents happened to be guiding the party. 'Look, it's fake', said Breton, rubbing his finger across the painted line on the glistening wall, 'the paint is still wet'. Truth to tell much of the Palaeolithic painting will smudge as the walls of the caves are often perennially wet.

Rouffignac and the problem of authenticity
The last case where the authenticity of painting was questioned was Rouffignac, announced to the world as a painted cave in 1956 by L. Nougier and R. Robert. The story illustrates well some of the problems of deciding the authenticity of cave art. The most unusual feature of Rouffignac is that it is a vast cavern with much wider and higher tunnels than is normal in the Dordogne region and the entrance has never been blocked. The passages wind altogether some eight kilometres and the entrance is only a few kilometres north of Les Eyzies. It was well known to speleologists and had been explored many times. As early as 1575 Francois de Belleforest noted: 'There are some altars there, and paintings in several places'. What the 'altars' were, and whether he was referring to the black paintings announced in 1956, is hard to be sure, but it does seem rather likely. This would make them genuine, because nobody would have faked them before 1575.

A round of dramatic announcements in July 1956, to the press and to the French prehistoric society congress taking place at the time, was

Right *A black painted bison, obscured by runs of stalactite guaranteeing its authenticity. It was first discovered in 1970 in the newly-opened 'Galerie Clastres' at Niaux.*

Left *The human figure rarely appears in cave art. This one, at Cougnac, has been speared.*

Below *A frieze of rhinos engraved along the cave wall at Rouffignac.*

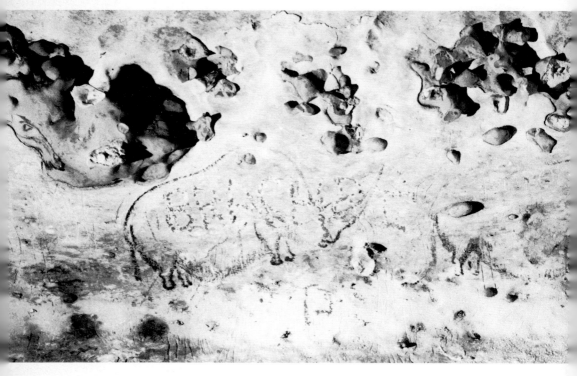

followed by a lot of acrimonious controversy, much of it irrelevant to the problem of authenticity. Then there was a visit by a party of international experts. One group, led by Breuil, came out in favour of unquestionable genuineness. Another, more cautious group asked for some analyses to be done, but subject to these being 'satisfactory' accepted the paintings' prehistoric origins. A third group signed nothing. These people are depicted in Nougier and Robert's book as skulking at the back of the party, casting dark glances around and hoping to discredit it all.

A degree of caution about Rouffignac is not unreasonable. Some caves are given good claims because they are newly discovered, through some formerly sealed entrance. For example a new gallery in Niaux was discovered in this way in 1970. Faking is thus usually ruled out. An important argument for the first few decades of research into ice age man was the presence of extinct animals amongst the subjects engraved or painted by early man. No faker could have convincingly done this. By about 1940, however, there were so many books on cave art that anyone could get hold of illustrations and copy them. Even so, a skilful detective should be able to spot which pictures have been copied and note errors in the faker's understanding of the style.

Rather more conclusive evidence of antiquity is provided by the thin runs of stalactite over the paintings in some caves like Cougnac. It seems impossible that these could form in less than a century or so; the exact rate of formation is poorly understood, and one crumbly form of stalactite does form very quickly, under concrete bridges for example. It may soon become routine to date stalactite formation by one of the uranium series techniques. Nevertheless the majority of cave paintings are sealed neither by stalactite nor by archaeological layers, and this is the case at Rouffignac.

There does seem to be a lot of painting and engraving in Rouffignac for anyone to have faked it all. In one or two places it does look a little unconvincing but many authentic caves have features in them that look 'odd'. Visitors who know about the controversy, including several parties of my own students, have come away convinced it is not genuine. But I suspect this is mainly a psychological effect; once the doubt has been sown the mind starts to look for evidence to confirm it. We are still a long way from having any concrete evidence either way.

In addition to the large number of black paintings and of engravings at Rouffignac, there are hundreds of metres of gallery with smearings and tracings on the ceiling. Archaeologists call this 'macaroni', and it is familiar in genuine painted caves. It seems improbable that this could be other than ancient. There are also some human heads which capture the feel of Palaeolithic art perfectly.

In the area of the so called 'foirail', or fair ground, deep inside the cave, there seems to be a contrast between the faded figures and the much more vivid black paintings over them. Maybe these newer and cruder looking paintings have been added recently, or maybe the whole decoration is genuinely Palaeolithic. Few writers on Palaeolithic art have chosen to stress Rouffignac, and to some extent doubts are likely to remain until some objective test is found.

The significance of cave art

Possibly one of the most remarkable things about Palaeolithic art is how little we can say about its meaning. We have had some success in dating it and much of it has been fully documented and beautifully photographed, especially by Jean Vertut. But people naturally ask to know more, to know why it was done, what it means and what it tells us about primitive man. After all it spans over twenty thousand years and is the prelude to, as well as the first two-thirds of, man's mastery of higher culture.

To the question why was it done there have been plenty of answers, mostly canvassed in the first decade of the century when cave art was first recognized. Some of them, like the view that art grew out of the leisure created by hunting success in a rich environment (the view of Lartet and Christy), that it came from the natural urge for adornment ('Art for art's sake' as Piette maintained) or that it sprang from man's recognition of fortuitous resemblances in nature, as Luquet claimed, are not really answers at more than a superficial level. Even the psychological theory that man needs art to help him overcome his anxieties about the world may be true but does not try to say why it is so. More concrete explanations concentrate on what the art was intended to achieve. Notable amongst these is the suggestion that it had some magical purpose, to help in the hunt or in pro-creation. There is certainly some evidence from caves like Montespan which is consistent with the hunting magic theory.

At a very prosaic level, it has been suggested that young hunters were shown the animal paintings to teach them what to hunt and how to kill it—hence the occasional spear in the pictures; in other words they were used in a sort of animal-recognition lesson. But the idea of penetrating deep into dangerous caves and using up precious lighting materials so unnecessarily is absurd. No one today seriously believes this is correct.

Strangely enough no one has ever considered whether the art is in some sense narrative. After all most medieval art told a story, usually biblical, and was intended to help instruct; quite a lot of ancient art is similarly narrative. Prehistoric pictures, too, could represent a story or myth, but if so it is too obscure for us to follow. People certainly do not figure very prominently in them and, whether narrative or not, this feature contrasts them sharply with most later art, which is people dominated.

Of the few books that make any positive contribution to the problems of cave art, by far the most original and penetrating is Siegfried Giedion's *The Eternal Present*. This beautifully designed book grew out of the A. W.

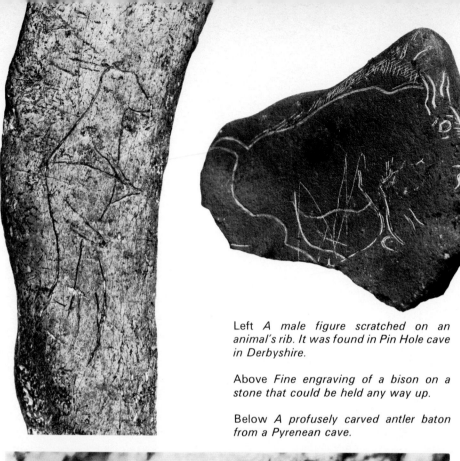

Left *A male figure scratched on an animal's rib. It was found in Pin Hole cave in Derbyshire.*

Above *Fine engraving of a bison on a stone that could be held any way up.*

Below *A profusely carved antler baton from a Pyrenean cave.*

Mellon lectures given in 1957. In it Giedion writes: 'Art born from ritual and magic; art born out of cosmic anguish; art as a sudden invention, rooted in the urge for adornment; art as an outcome of man's urge to play; art for art's sake: all these theories, and maybe still others contain some element of truth. The urge for art cannot be limited to a single impulse. The nature of the dominant impulse will change according to man's concepts of the world.'

The idea that a single factor could explain all Palaeolithic art is an oddly naïve one, implausible to anyone familiar with art. Of the proponents of the various views on the motivation for cave art, it is particularly notable that none of them has ever suggested that all the other explanations are wrong; indeed most have been commendably cautious in their conclusions.

It is extremely unlikely that the Palaeolithic artist was like the modern concept of an artist—a rebel and a recluse, keeping apart from society and mistrusting it. In latter-day primitive society, art has been part of everyday life and artists integral members of society, expressing its hopes and fears, enjoying its full backing and appreciation; in this sense the primitive artist is poles apart from van Gogh.

The question why the prehistoric art was done is probably misconceived. Primitive artists have been asked such questions, and have expressed puzzlement, even disbelief. To them the answer is that it is their way. An anthropologist might add that for them it has probably always been their way, at least back for the several generations they know of. They may hope for some positive result, like hunting success; but this is more or less incidental. Prehistorians might conclude that the astonishing continuity of cave art over more than 20,000 years was equally due to the simple fact that it was their way.

The question we should really be asking is that asked by Giedion. What does primeval art tell us about early man's view of the world? Here we may briefly touch on just two of Giedion's remarkable insights, man's view of his role in the world, and his space conception.

The art contains good clues concerning man's relationship with the animal world. The animals are executed with exquisite skill and occupy the centre of the stage; the humans are, to put it mildly, scruffy little figures. The animals were the gods of the world of early man. 'In the zoomorphic period,' writes Giedion, 'the figure of the human being appeared negligible in comparison with the beauty and strength of the animal figure. The unequal relationship can be observed in the scanty representations of human beings left by prehistoric man. The self-adulation with which both male and female nudes were presented in the sunlight of Greek sculpture were totally unimaginable for primeval man.'

Secondly there is the idea of space. Both on portable objects, which after all can be held any way up, and on the ceilings and walls of the caves, the animals are at all angles to one another. Vertical and horizontal hardly exist, though we are always tempted to straighten the picture to fit our convention of horizontality. Of this space concept, Giedion says: 'It is not chaos. It approaches rather to the order of the stars, which move about in endless space, unconfined and universal in their relations. Violent juxtapositions in size as well as time were accepted as a matter of course. All was displayed within an eternal present, the perpetual interflow of today, yesterday and tomorrow'.

Decorated pieces and the dating of cave art

The dating of Palaeolithic art depends on objects found in dated archaeological layers. These can be large blocks of engraved limestone, or tiny stone statuettes, or engraved stone plaques. Decorated antler and bone objects are common, many of them believed to be functional, such as spear throwers, disc-buttons, perforated batons, spatulas and half-round rods. Painted pieces are rare. The only additional datable works are bas reliefs, engravings and paintings on walls which are actually covered by dated deposits or are in caves known to have been sealed at a particular time. These must be contemporary with or older than their burial or sealing. Sometimes, as for example in the baked terracottas from Dolni Vestonice, they are obviously no older than the hut, with its little baking oven, in which they were found.

No representational art has been found in a Mousterian context or in the first phase of the Upper Palaeolithic in western Europe. But carved and, occasionally, painted blocks are found all through the succeeding Aurignacian layers, from the earliest of about 33,000 BC to the latest of about 26,000 BC. A rather smaller number of art pieces are found in central Europe in association with the culture called Szeletian of 25,000 to 40,000 BC.

No doubt in some cases the limestone blocks which make up the majority of Aurignacian dated art have broken off the cliff walls since they were carved. The oldest painting seems to be from the Castanet rock shelter. It is the black outline of the head of a wild ox; it is from what seems to be the earliest Aurignacian level on the Dordogne. The style of painting is, frankly, crude but two painted blocks from a much later Aurignacian level, of about 27,000 BC, in the Ferrassie rock shelter are much like it. Even a painted deer head from the succeeding culture phase (Noaillan), found at Labattut rock shelter, exhibits a technique of painting which has improved little by about 25,000 BC.

The style of engraving is similarly crude in the earlier Aurignacian, before about 30,000 BC. The technique of engraving seems to begin with a pecked line which, in the second half of the Aurignacian, is definitely replaced by a finer line technique, probably accomplished by skilful use of the burin. A relief carving technique is also later found. Ferrassie rock

150

A baked clay 'venus' from Dolni Vestonice in Czechoslovakia has, in common with other such Palaeolithic figurines, been regarded as reflecting a pre-occupation with fertility.

151

Right *A 'venus' from a Mediterranean Riviera cave at Grimaldi. The buttocks exhibit a fatty enlargement, called steatopygia, that is found today among Bushman women.*

Below *The vulvar symbol appears in different forms in Palaeolithic art. It may also indicate a concern with fertility. Left, from Abri du Poisson, dates from 32,000 years ago; centre, from la Ferrassie, from 28,000 years ago; right, from Pergouset, from 14,000 years ago.*

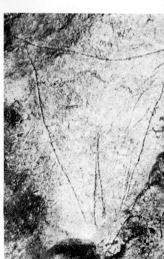

shelter has some of the best evidence of this later development. Crudeness of technique is entirely to be expected in the first groping stages of art, but they are poor dating evidence, since unfinished works or the work of incompetents of any subsequent date could be confused with the true primitive work.

A characteristic feature of Aurignacian art is the vulvar symbol which is more frequently found than any other subject, from the earliest to the latest sites. In the earliest stages vulvar symbols are pear-shaped, while in the later Aurignacian a sub-triangular shape becomes more common. There are also examples of phalluses, some engraved on stone and one from the Blanchard rock shelter finely carved in the round in bison horn.

A vulvar of characteristic late Aurignacian style is found on the earliest of a series of statuettes of the succeeding period. This is the limestone 'venus' from Willendorf in lower Austria, dating from about 27,000 BC, close to the end of the Aurignacian art period of the Dordogne. A number of rudimentary statuettes are known from Aurignacian France, but the earliest examples are animals from the south German site of Vogelherd; the best are a horse, a mammoth and a lion. None of the venus statuettes are known to be earlier than Willendorf. In France they seem to belong to the Noaillan (about 26,000 to 20,000 BC); the central European examples are about the same age, while in Russia some are rather later. Their distinctive features are remarkably consistent. All are plump, if not actually overtly pregnant. The buttocks are large and accentuated; in a few cases they resemble the condition called steatopygia, a fatty extension backwards of the buttocks found in the females of the Bushman peoples. The breasts are large, also suggestive of pregnancy. By contrast, facial features are rare. In no cases are the eyes, nose and mouth all shown. The arms are slender and often folded over the breasts. The thighs are well formed, but the legs taper and the feet are rarely included. Many authors have argued that the vulvar symbols, phalluses and 'venuses' indicate an interest in, if not obsession with, fertility; no plausible alternative view has been advanced.

The peoples who lived in the Dordogne between 26,000 and 13,000 BC failed to leave behind much datable art, but enough survives to suggest that art was more or less continuously practised. It also confirms that the basic canons of style changed little during the entire span of cave art. In addition to the venuses which give a characteristic stamp to Noaillan art in western Europe, there are several fine engravings like the horse on the bone spearhead from Isturitz (Basses Pyrénées). These seem to be an improvement on anything found in the Aurignacian and one has the impression that the standard and style of the engraving is practically intermediate between the first engravings, of around 30,000 BC, and the great majority of dated engravings, from the later Magdalenian, after 13,000 BC, which are usually very refined.

The other two dated pieces, which shine out like search lights from this dark age in the evolution of cave art, are the bas reliefs of Roc de Sers and Fourneau du Diable. They are very impressive and forcefully contradict the idea that art had universally fallen to a low ebb; on the other hand they are not easy to compare with paintings or even engravings. Their similarity to the Magdalenian bas reliefs is disconcerting.

For Leroi-Gourhan, they belong to an archaic phase. With them he places Lascaux, Pech Merle and Cougnac. He makes a special point of the similarity between the Lascaux bulls and those from the dated slab of Fourneau du Diable. There is also a similarity between the ibexes of Roc de Sers and ibexes in the axial gallery of Lascaux facing each other either side of a tectiform. Possible dates for this early style, if it really is earlier than the main Magdalenian style are 20,000 to 25,000 BC or 16,000 to 19,000 BC or 13,000 to 16,000 BC. It could span all three periods, or, as Leroi-Gourhan maintains, the last two only—later Solutrian and earlier Magdalenian. The dating of Lascaux depends on this issue; a radiocarbon assay suggests early Magdalenian.

Magdalenian art

Art dated to the Magdalenian, mainly from about 13,000 to 9,000 BC is much more abundant than that of earlier times. In fact four exceptionally rich sites, la Madeleine and Laugerie Basse in the Dordogne, and Mas d'Azil (Ariège) and Isturitz in the Pyrenees, have probably given us a better sample of high art than many hunting cultures which survived to recent times.

The most distinctive traits of Magdalenian art are as usual the symbols. The fish tail vulvas are distinctive; a variety of penises have been shown, indicating circumcision or even the more drastic mutilations known as sub-incision; and barbed signs, phallic according to Leroi-Gourhan, are also to my knowledge unknown before the Magdalenian.

A more general stylistic trait, typical of the animal pictures, is 'shading', both in painting and engraving. The manes of the horses display the technique especially clearly. In engraving, a series of closely spaced fine lines or hachures is employed; in painting, a series of fine painted lines. The beards of the horses and bison are often similarly hachured. There is much subtle shading on the bodies, simulating fur, and usually placed on the stomach, shoulders or hind quarters. Such shading is not however universal. A very fine line technique without shading is used on engravings from Teyjat and Limeuil (both Dordogne).

On the other hand, these details apart, the overall conventions of Magdalenian art are so similar to those used back to Aurignacian times that simple figures are always going to be difficult to date. The Magdalenians probably came across earlier art pieces, and they may have revered such

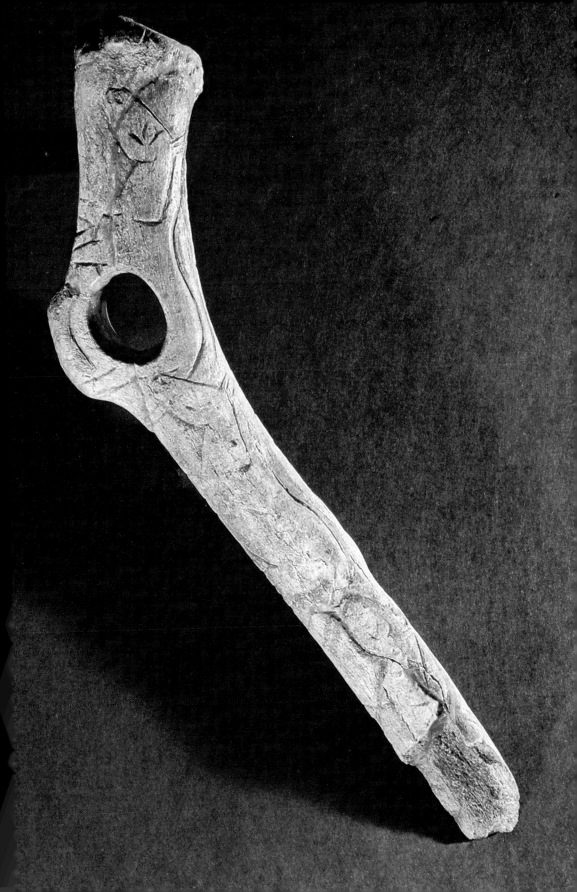

Two reindeer carved on antler from Bruniquel. A close observation of the animals around him is apparent from all the painting, engraving and modelling left by ice age man.

Previous page A perforated baton of the type called in French 'baton de commandement'. For nineteenth century 'functional' archaeologists they were 'shaft-straighteners'.

156

ancient work and consciously kept to its conventions, in the way that New Kingdom Egypt copied the conventions of the Old Kingdom, to reinforce a claim to the land and heritage.

The human figure

Before the Magdalenian, the only major representation of the human figure is in the venus figurines. It is questionable if their style is reproduced in wall art, though I think the female figures smeared on the clay of the ceiling of Pech Merle belong to this series. The speared men of Cougnac and Pech Merle may also be of pre-Magdalenian date.

Many more human figures date from the Magdalenian; they are common on dated objects, and enable us to date the remainder, which are on the walls. Stylized female figures, like the statuette from Petersfels in south-west Germany and the engravings on a limestone block from Lalinde (Dordogne), are characteristic of the late part of the Magdalenian. In engravings these are always shown in side view. They have concave or at

A human figure with a bison's head and tail could be a disguised man or a half-human, half-bison god. The object in his mouth may be a musical bow or a flute.

A mysterious engraved scene from Addaura in Sicily is about 12,000 years old. Some of the figures seem to be dancing while others are bound; they may be taking part in a circumcision or initiation ritual.

158

least flat stomachs which distinguish them from the plumper venuses of pre-Magdalenian date. Breasts are sometimes shown, but are not particularly distended and often small or absent altogether. The only systematically emphasized parts are the buttocks, which protrude backwards. The figures are often 'bent' or angled at the waist in a boomerang shape. The head is rarely shown, and the feet and arms are equally unimportant. In some cases, as at Lalinde, there is a deep incised line across the abdomen as seen in side view, roughly on the axis of the vagina; this may have some sexual significance.

There is an important series of male figures, though only a few are explicitly shown as males by the inclusion of the penis. Some of the clearest have animal attributes: bison horns as at Gabillou (Dordogne), or antlers such as those engraved on the painted figure from les Trois Frères. In some cases tails, claws, animal ears and beards are added. Sometimes the posture is explicitly animal, the body being oblique or horizontal; often the body is shaded in the same way that animal fur was shown. The bison men are the most common and seem to be Magdalenian.

Other probable male heads seem to be masked or cartoon-like. These heads grade into others that are sometimes called ghosts from their unreal appearance. In the whole range there is not a single human figure depicted in a fully upright posture, with definite human facial features or with the kind of care lavished on the animals. This is the basis for Giedion's estimate of the role of man in the Palaeolithic world view. Men depict themselves only rarely but animals constantly; they seem to want to be animals and lacked any arrogance in their humanity.

Cave art was therefore a continuous tradition for more than 20,000 years in the late Palaeolithic of western Europe. But what of the hunting bands that engendered it? How numerous where they? How long did they live? Where did they live? How did they survive? What food, clothing or shelter was available to them?

Chapter VII Hunting Societies

Life expectancy

Estimates of the life expectancy of early man are based mainly on the evidence of skeletons. Age at death may be determined from the state of eruption of the teeth or from the fusion of the ends of the bones. A weakness in the procedure arises from the possibility that the timing of eruption and fusion may have been different in prehistoric times; if the neoteny theory is correct many of these changes may have occurred earlier in the body than they do now and we could be over-estimating the ages of prehistoric skeletons.

Figures for the expectancy of life usually exclude infant mortality. This is just as well because infant bones are more fragile, less likely to survive, and certain to be under-represented. There is little direct evidence of infant death in the Palaeolithic but, even when medical science first came into contact with non-literate societies, the figure for infant mortality was regularly over 20 per cent. For hunters the figure is not likely to be under 50 per cent, and if infanticide is included it is probably much more. Among baboons, which are analogous to early man in being open-country primates at risk from predators, levels of 80 per cent are recorded. The Neanderthal burials at la Ferrassie, where two adults are found with one child and four infants or newly-borns, would be consistent with an infant mortality of half or more.

According to figures compiled by H. V. Vallois, the average longevity for Neanderthals was 29·4 years—not exactly a ripe old age. This means roughly half the people lived beyond this age, while roughly half did not reach it. The figure for the Cromagnon men of the Upper Palaeolithic was 32 years, and for the 'Mesolithic' hunters living since the last ice age the figure was 31. Before feeling too sorry about the low expectancy of life of these folk, one should remember that longevity of only 30 to 40 years was normal everywhere down to the last few hundred years and the impact of medicine. So Palaeolithic people lived about as long as more recent populations; they were probably also fitter and healthier. There are cases in recent hunting societies where it is claimed that individuals quite commonly lived to over sixty but most of them lived no longer than the Cromagnons.

Some data also exists on the very first hominids based on the number of individuals whose third molars (wisdom teeth) had come through; today this happens between eighteen and twenty but it was probably rather earlier two million years ago. In the gracile species *africanus* 65 per cent had survived until the third molar came through, implying survival beyond the age of eighteen, perhaps with a life expectancy of twenty or twenty-five. The robust species did not live as long; only 43 per cent lived until their third molars erupted, and their life expectancy was accordingly under eighteen and perhaps under fifteen. This is the sort of figure found in non-human species. Even the percentage of early hominids living until the eruption of their second molar at about twelve years was small: 57 per cent for *robustus* and 75 per cent for *africanus*.

In surviving hunting societies women have children on average every four years, while more settled farmers average a child every two years. Child-bearing is possible for some sixteen years so that a couple of hunters would average four children. If infant mortality were high or infanticide practised, they would probably do little more than maintain their numbers with two surviving children. If, however, anything in excess of two surviving children were maintained over long periods, say 2·1 on average, the population would rise.

World population

In 1960, Edward Deevey, in an article in *Scientific American* called 'The Human Population', gave estimates of 5·32 million, 3·24 million, 1 million and 125,000 for the population of the world 10,000, 25,000, 300,000 and 1,000,000 years ago respectively. His over-all average densities for these early hunting societies were based on comparisons with surviving primitive societies. The population one million years ago was calculated on the area of Africa alone; the area of the entire Old World was used thereafter; the New World was added when calculating for 10,000 years ago. In 1960 it was still thought that the first men emerged one million years ago at the earliest; today we would guess at over two million years.

Deevey converted these population figures into an estimate for the total number of hunters in human history. But the figures should be recalculated for several reasons. In the first place some estimate is needed for the population before one million years ago. Secondly it now seems very likely that the average density of population in most occupied areas during the Upper Palaeolithic increased to rather more than Deevey's four hunters per hundred square kilometres.

Left *A Masai tribesman stalking through the east African savannah. The hunting way of life habitual among all men for 99 per cent of human history has largely been abandoned in favour of farming.*

Below *Ice age man portrayed the fishes and birds which probably supplemented his diet as they do that of surviving modern-day hunters.*

Thirdly it is possible to attempt to refine the estimates of the area occupied. For example, Deevey took Africa as a whole with thirty million square kilometres. But it now seems that the entire rainforest sector was not at first occupied; and that, during arid periods, most of the Sahara remained unoccupied. It is now also possible to be a little more precise about the time when areas like Siberia were first occupied. Even with such refinements, it is obvious that the whole venture is highly speculative. The important point is that there are a surprising number of lines of evidence which help to qualify it.

My revised estimates for world population of hunters are obtained simply by multiplying the estimated density of hunters for each period by the revised figure for the area occupied. This model allows for a high density at the end of the Palaeolithic, a medium density of four hunters per hundred square kilometres for the earlier Palaeolithic and a still lower density before one million years ago. An alternative model would allow the small-bodied early hominids a higher density; such higher densities are found among baboons, the most comparable open-country primate group, and it certainly could be argued that more smaller-bodied individuals could be supported per square kilometre than bigger hunters.

The above data gives us a revised estimate for the cumulative total of all people in the world, hunters and non-hunters. I suspect that such a total should be visualized as excluding most of those who failed to survive infancy. A figure of 40,000 to 50,000 million for post-glacial food-producing societies is known to be of the right order. The figure for the last million years of hunting societies is less than Deevey's 66 billion (1 billion = 1,000 million), which seems to be too high (due to the mistaken addition of 30 billion instead of 3 billion for his 'Mesolithic'), but a little higher than the corrected figure of 39 billion. A better figure seems to be in the order of 45 to 60 billion, perhaps 50 billion. To this must be added 5 to 20 billion for the tool makers, of before one million years ago. We arrive at a total for hunters of around 60 billion and for food-producing societies of about 45 billion, of whom $3\frac{1}{2}$ billion live today. The grand total is a little over 100 billion and rather over half were hunters, which is not surprising when one remembers that for over 99 per cent of human history farming was unknown.

Hunting bands
Time and again, in attempting to reconstruct the way of life of Palaeolithic man, evidence is brought forward of the life-style of recent hunters. Where the prehistoric situation is not revealed by direct, archaeological evidence, which would otherwise take priority, it is certainly sensible to discover what similarities there might feasibly have been between past and present hunters. Conclusions drawn from such ethnographic parallels are very far from proof however.

Estimates of the size of prehistoric hunting bands rely particularly heavily upon comparisons with present-day practice. Hunters tend to live in small groups of restricted geographical range. Among a recent sample of 53 Old World hunting societies the average was 25 persons in each band. Only about 7 per cent of hunters are to any degree sedentary, the remainder are consistently nomadic. This is mainly due to sparseness of food supply, which ensures that half of all hunter bands do not exceed 50 persons throughout the year.

Normally the male is the hunter of animals, while the female, often burdened with children and less mobile, is the hunter of plants, or gatherer. Both share the surplus they bring home, which has an important effect on the relationship between male and female. 18 per cent of a sample were strictly monogamous; 47 per cent were monogamous with occasional polygamy. 36 per cent were polygamous. Nearly half the groups were required to marry outside their band; all were prevented by incest tabus from marrying close relatives. Hunters, possibly because they are usually nomadic and have to travel light, have little personal property; nor do they normally accumulate food surpluses.

Diet

The question of what early man ate and how he acquired it is of great interest. For most animals the entire economy is based on the quest for food and this must have been early man's principal preoccupation.

Let us first consider the relative proportions of food derived from animal and vegetable sources. It is evident from the abundant bones left in caves and other occupation sites that animals were eaten in large numbers. But there is only the most minimal archaeological evidence of vegetable food. It would be unwise however to assume that this is a fair reflection of the true situation.

In a recent and most useful monograph on hunters, called *Man the Hunter* and edited by Lee and DeVore, it was pointed out that many of them derive 70 to 80 per cent of their food from vegetable sources. Accordingly one school has taken to saying that the so-called hunters of prehistoric times, whose remains are found in deposits with animals bones, were really vegetable-food gatherers and only a small proportion of their food came from hunting.

The true situation among recent hunters seems to be a little more complicated. Taking the average of a large sample of 58 hunting societies from all parts of the world, the percentage of vegetable food is 39. More importantly this percentage changes with latitude; the tropical latitude hunter-gatherers have a specially high vegetable-food content in their diet, but never apparently over 80 per cent. The middle latitudes see a more equal proportion of the two components—animal- and plant-food. Hunters in the high (colder) latitudes, in the equivalent of the environment of the reindeer hunters of the ice ages eat as little as 10 per cent vegetable-food or less.

Presumably it is more realistic to compare the ice age hunters of Europe and northern Asia with the predominantly meat- and fish-eating peoples of high latitudes; while the early hunters of east Africa should presumably be compared with today's tropical peoples. But there is a paradox here for people like the Hadza, living near lake Eyasi in Tanzania, are reported to eat only 20 per cent meat yet live in a region with some of the most abundant game in the world.

The animal-food component of a hunter's diet is not all made up of hunted mammals. Fish and birds are included. Towards the equator reptiles, amphibians and invertebrates can be added. Shell fish and other edible molluscs are important to some coastal economies. Our distant early primate and pre-primate ancestors probably mainly ate insects; some tropical hunters continue to relish them.

Shells of edible molluscs are well represented archaeologically. Fish remains are more rarely found on Palaeolithic sites; this may be due to bad preservation or to inadequate techniques of excavation and sieving.

Vegetable-food traces are exceedingly rarely found in the Palaeolithic. Peking man at Choukoutien, and the Acheulians at Orgnac (Ardèche) and other sites ate the hackberry; its stones fossilize easily and are found in limestone sites. Hazel nuts are sometimes found, as at Taubach near Weimar. The excavators of the Derbyshire cave of Pin Hole claimed to have found a duck egg, opened at one end, from the late Palaeolithic levels, along with bones of sole, roach and pike. But with the rapid decomposition of most vegetable matter discoveries of this kind are bound to remain rare.

Potentially valuable techniques like analysis of fossil excreta or of the biochemistry of the human bone, which might indicate diet, are still only at a provisional stage. Human excreta from Terra Amata, near Nice, apparently indicated a meat diet.

Among modern hunters malnutrition and starvation are rare. Death more often comes through infanticide, accident, murder or cannibalism.

Hunting
Much of a hunter's life is taken up with the hunt itself, or with the preparation for it. From early childhood, he begins to prepare himself, learning the characteristics of the animals and the difficulties of catching them. Parents or elder brothers and sisters pass on to the younger members of the family the skills of food-getting. Finally, on initiation to adulthood, the young person acquires a sense of pride in the ability to be self-sufficient, to hunt or to gather and to rear children. A great deal of prestige is attached to being a successful hunter. Possibly the most important factor in the social

status of a hunter is his success in presenting his relatives with the prescribed and time-honoured gifts of choice portions of meat.

The problems of reconstructing the techniques of hunting used by prehistoric man are great. We have already noted that spears are known from before the last glaciation, for example at the site of the elephant kill at Lehringen. A giant deer from near Roermond in Holland had a stone spear point lodged in its lower jaw. The hole in a reindeer scapula from Meiendorf near Hamburg exactly matched the size of the barbed harpoon heads used there. A bison scapula from the Yenisei river region in Siberia had been pierced by a spear point of reindeer antler. The hole made by a wooden spear was found in the pelvis of a Mount Carmel Neanderthal.

Among recent hunters, a variety of pit-falls and traps were regularly used. At Olduvai, in prehistoric times, bovids appear to have been driven into a marsh and killed. And many sites with stone tools and animal bones, like Swanscombe, or travertine spring sites, like Ehringsdorf, near Weimar, are likely to have been watering places for animals, suitable for ambush or even poisoning. Nevertheless, positive evidence for trapping game is not known from any prehistoric site.

The clearest known evidence for hunting ritual comes from the cave of Montespan (Haute Garonne), not far from les Trois Frères cave, with its antlered 'shaman'. The clay-covered wall has been crudely incised with the figure of a horse. Then some pointed object with a conical end has been repeatedly jabbed into its body, leaving it riddled with holes.

Elsewhere in the cave, and made fairly inaccessible by a 'siphon', or underwater neck of the cave, was a model of an animal roughly-shaped in clay. Clearly it was intended to be a bear, for a real bear skull was found at its head; evidently the pelt of a bear with skull attached had been stretched over the clay body. The model had been repeatedly stabbed.

The first burials

The practice of burial goes back to Neanderthal man. In fact the main reason why we have Neanderthal skeletons as opposed to isolated skull bits is that organized burial gives the whole skeleton a much better chance of surviving. Since the burials are mainly found in living areas, the absence of them in some cultures might actually indicate a more practical people; the risks of infection must be increased by burial of possibly infected dead near where animals are cut up for food. Later peoples have tended to bury their dead away from the living area.

Burials become common by about 15,000 BC, but their incidence before that, back to about 60,000 BC when we are first sure they exist, is very patchy. By Neanderthal times, from about 60,000 BC, men were carefully excavating a grave, sometimes to a depth of 50 centimetres, and placing inside it the body, accompanied by objects and even, apparently, by food.

166

It is a widely-held opinion that careful burial reflects an entirely new attitude to life and death from that prevailing in pre-human times and that amongst apes and monkeys who leave their dead unceremoniously where they fall. The usual view is that it implies belief in an after-life and the desire to see that the dead person goes to it. This seems a reasonable interpretation, given the wide survival of such a belief in recent times.

Another suggestion might be that man had become sufficiently sensitive for the idea of death and dead bodies to trouble him, whereas, before, it had not been of great concern. Pained by seeing the dead exposed or attacked by carnivores, he started to bury them if only to get them out of sight and safe from damage.

Death and burial is not an everyday occurrence in a small hunting band. It is as special a time as the other 'life-crisis' rites of birth, puberty and marriage. It represents a rare break from routine. The routine of a hunter's life may have been less monotonous and soul-destroying than that of a peasant tied to the land or of a factory worker but he may have increasingly welcomed opportunities to meet his fellows. Hunters with a low density of population can usually congregate in groups of more than a dozen no more than a few times a year. The ritual and ceremony which go with primitive funerals provide such an opportunity.

Burials are very much the archaeologist's stock-in-trade. Without them we would have no Tutankhamun, no jade princess, and no Sutton Hoo, even though in this latter case custom had gone so far that even the absence of the body made little difference. Burials are certainly a useful source of evidence for the Palaeolithic.

Most Neanderthal burials were accompanied by what are believed to be grave goods. However, because these grave goods are all so simple, they are all individually open to some doubt. The 'three fine flints' with the Ferrassie V child are not proven gifts; they might just have happened to be lying about when the burial was made. The 'leg of bison' from la Chapelle is intriguing because only the lower leg bones were found and these were still in anatomical connection. Clearly the flesh and skin had still been on the bones and holding them together when they were buried with the old man. The meaty part of a leg is higher up but the lower part with a few scraps on it could be used for little more than soup. Were they being parsimonious?

Taken as a whole, the Neanderthal grave goods list can only be interpreted as evidence that it was normal in the Neanderthal-Mousterian period to put objects with burials for some symbolic or religious purpose. As far as we know this practice began no earlier than the last interglacial. It became typical in the block of time immediately preceding the Upper Palaeolithic-Cromagnon period along with other indications of ritual and ideology. It is therefore another argument for continuity between the Neanderthals and the Cromagnons.

Cromagnon burials

Cromagnon burials, dating from 35,000 to 10,000 BC, are known from more than twenty-five sites across Europe into Siberia. Some are multiple burials as at Predmost in Czechoslovakia where more than twenty bodies were discovered and as many as forty persons may be represented. A triple burial was found at Barma Grande, one of the Grimaldi caves in Italy. But most are single.

We would like to know whether there were any specific repeated rites of burial at this time; both the geographical and the time spread make this difficult. The practice of contraction is quite common, a procedure usually involving tying the body so that the knees were drawn up to the chest. Explanations vary from the ideological, that the person was going to be reborn and was buried in the foetal position, to the prosaic, that a smaller grave would suffice for a trussed corpse. Tight contraction is unknown in the Neanderthal burials, though several were slightly flexed. But, among the Cromagnons, contractions were more common than extended burials. Amongst the Neanderthals, burials in a supine position on the back were as common as those on left or right, while in Cromagnons this position is quite frequently found. A group of late Magdalenian adult burials from south-west France, in the period 9,000 to 13,000 BC, were all buried crouched on their left side; this suggests a standardization of practice at that time.

Perhaps the most striking fact about Cromagnon burials is the frequency with which they were strewn with red ochre. Sometimes it was apparent that buckets-full had been used; the bones and the whole grave area were stained, as is true of some occupation sites. In a sample of 30 Cromagnon burials, 22 were ochre-strewn.

True cremations are unknown in Europe or Asia, but partial cremations are known from Grimaldi, from Czechoslovakia and from the Russian site of Sungir where coals had singed the body. The earliest-known true cremation is from Mungo Lake in New South Wales and dates from about 25,000 BC. Further evidence from Australia may throw light on this surprising find.

Adornment

Much of our information about the adornment and clothes that the living Cromagnons wore comes from burials where beads, necklaces and other trinkets are frequently found still in position on the body, giving the best available guide to how they were worn.

More often found than any other form of adornment are head-dresses, usually indicated by rows of beads of antler or ivory or perforated teeth or shells. These may perhaps have decorated fur caps or the like which would have helped Palaeolithic man survive the cold winters. They are equally

Previous page *A double burial of* Homo sapiens *at Sungir, north-east of Moscow. The first deliberate burials date from about 60,000 years ago.*

Right *Carving of a horse found buried with the bodies at Sungir.*

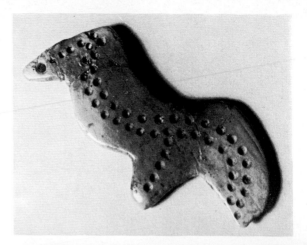

Right *Some sort of head-dress appears to crown this small ivory carving from Brassempouy.*

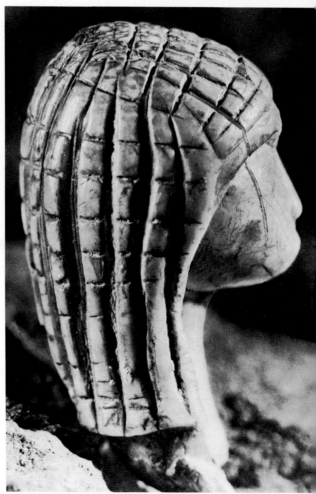

typical of Russia, Italy and south-west France.

Necklaces or collars were not unknown, but the sample I have followed up included only 7 necklaces against 18 head-dresses. There are also examples of waist-bands or belts, including a kind of buckle from the Siberian site of Malta. Wrist, elbow, knee and ankle adornments were all rare, but a youth buried at la Madeleine had all of these.

Beads and similar adornment are also found away from burials, but in such cases their purpose is much less clear. For example, a little perforated bear figurine from Isturitz may or may not have been a pendant or an amulet. The first appearance of perforated beads coincides in many areas, such as France, Italy and central Europe, with the beginning of the Upper Palaeolithic or more precisely 'Leptolithic' blade technology. This seems to fit the model of the more playful and child-like disposition which, we have earlier hypothesized, begins with Cromagnon man.

Clothes

As far as we know, woven cloth was first made in post-Palaeolithic times, though simple plaiting of reeds or naturally available fibres could have been practised earlier. In the Palaeolithic it is likely that skin clothes were worn; one of the consolations of hunting in a cold climate is that one's prey tends to have an attractive fur coat easily borrowed when the animal is butchered. Very probably the first men to colonize the temperate to cold zone at the end of the *erectus* period initiated the use of skin cloaks. Towards the close of the Palaeolithic clear evidence of a major development in the exploitation of skins emerges in the form of fine-eyed needles of bone and more numerous and finer piercers of flint. In south-west France they appear abruptly at about 17,000 BC in the late Solutrian; they may have been invented at that time or they may be a little earlier at sites further east like Predmost and Sungir.

Sungir is one of the most informative of burial sites and provides good evidence of clothing. Even more rare, it is almost alone in having been discovered and carefully excavated in the last twenty-five years. The site is on the outskirts of Vladimir, some 200 kilometres east-north-east of Moscow, and accordingly one of the most northerly we know. The burial of a man, Sungir I, was found in 1964 by the Soviet archaeologist Otto Bader; further burials were found in 1969, but full details are not yet available in English.

The clothing was reconstructed on the basis of a row of beads; clearly they had been sewn on to skin garments. The man had been wearing a skin 'shirt' and trousers. The shirt had rows of beads passing right across the front and round the back; evidently it was a sort of poncho. The trousers had rows of beads down the legs. These continued on to the shoes, suggesting that the leather shoes were attached to the trousers like moccasins.

171

The man probably wore a fur hat, possibly attached to his coat like the hood of an anorak. Several skin cloaks seem to have been thrown over him as well as piles of ochre and coals.

It is very probable that burials with beads at wrists, elbows, ankles and knees, as at la Madeleine, also betray skin suits. But the most clear-cut evidence of tailoring is surely that of the little statuettes, presumably female, from two sites in the lake Baikal region of southern Siberia. The best is from Buret and three rather poorer specimens come from Malta. They have a radiocarbon date of 12,800 BC but their true age may be a little earlier. Evidently these people made true tailored skin suits, covering the whole body, in the manner of the eskimos; it is possible that there were two layers with fur inside and outside for maximum protection and comfort.

There are some clues to clothing from cave art. Although the venuses of Europe, unlike Siberia, seem to be naked, there are traces on the backs of some of them of a kind of waist-band. The male figure with the Laussel venuses seems to have a belt and, judging by the absence of any representation of the penis, was probably meant to be wearing trousers.

Some possibly clothed figures are known in engravings from Isturitz and Montastruc in the Pyrenees, both of late Magdalenian date. A bone piece from Isturitz has two crawling figures on it. Bands are clearly shown round their wrists, neck and ankles and look like the fringes of an overall suit; but the front figure has breasts shown so it may be that the bands are loose and are simply decorative. A tall poorly-drawn figure from Montastruc, seen in front view, seems to have a row of no less than seven buttons down his front. It seems likely that these are a representation of the button-like discs which occur in archaeological assemblages of this period. They are small rondels of bone, cut out of the scapula, perforated in the centre and often finely engraved with animal figures.

The group of paintings which tells us most about the clothes worn by hunters is the Spanish Levant series, generally thought to date from after the ice age, but probably reflecting hunters' dress of milder climates. Head-dresses are their most characteristic feature. Some are obviously made of a few feathers, others are tall and shown as a block, perhaps representing the kind of head-dress with closely-packed feathers worn by Red Indian chiefs. Some figures have trousers to the knees and a kind of fringe decoration is common at the knee. A fringe at the waist is also found. The sites of Cogul (Lerida), Alpera (Albacete) and Dos Aguas (Valencia) show us early female fashion: the women have long skirts of mid-calf length, somewhat bell-shaped and suspended from the waist; their breasts hang loose and the effect is that of the Minoan style.

Three hearths in the floor of the Palaeolithic hut at Pincevent. Stone 'seats' lie beside two of them. The entire plan of the hut is shown on page 185.

Previous page *The Volgu blade. One of a cache of leaf-shaped points, made by pressure flaking in the Solutrian style, that was found in eastern France. It is the most spectacular tool of the Palaeolithic.*

174

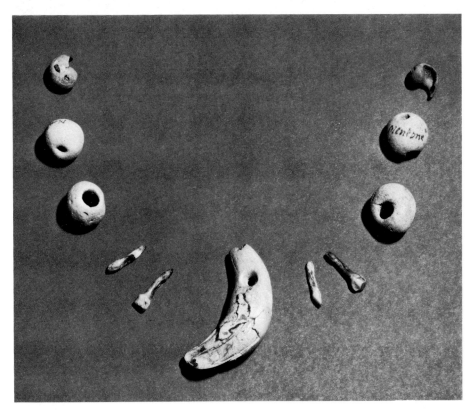

Above *The many perforated teeth and beads and shells that are found in ice age deposits, on the hut floor at Pincevent for instance, were probably linked at one time into necklaces.*

Below *The glutton engraved on this bone pendant from the Dordogne is a small carnivore now inhabiting only the northern forests.*

Music

Evidence of music in the Palaeolithic is in the form of bone flutes and whistles. In addition oval pendants are found which are probably bull-roarers, designed to produce a whirring sound and favoured in magical ceremonies. Some of the perforated bone batons resemble the drum sticks used by the shaman in Lapland.

The bone tubes with spaced holes, believed to be flutes, are common in the early Upper Palaeolithic but rare later. In fact the only Magdalenian example comes from an early Magdalenian context, and the late Magdalenian, with so much other evidence of advanced culture, has none. The cave of le Placard produced a complex four-piece flute, believed to be a sort of pan-pipe. A Russian example contemporary with the Magdalenian is from the Molodova site in the Dniestr; it is a long pipe of elk horn with six finger-holes.

The majority of the flutes are earlier than 20,000 BC. Central European examples made by bear hunters used the long bones of young bears, perforated with three to five finger-holes, unless one hole is a sounding hole. The French examples are made on bird bones, in one case on the leg of a vulture. Three or four holes are normal. Because they are all damaged it is difficult to know what kind of mouth piece they had or how they were blown. They seem to date from between 20,000 and 30,000 BC. Whistles, usually made by a single perforation on a phalange bone, are also common, especially in the Magdalenian. They may have been used for signalling in hunts. It is possible that the flutes were used for 'charming' animals with a view to killing them.

An engraving from les Trois Frères shows a bison-man, with an object in his mouth. Possibly it is a flute. Others have suggested that it might be a musical bow such as the Bushmen use, holding one end in the mouth and twanging the string.

Dwellings

The only major category of archaeological evidence indicating the size of Palaeolithic social groups is won from calculation of the area of the sites they occupied. The floor area of a hut is the best example, but it would also be useful to know what area of a cave mouth was occupied. Ethnography provides some estimates of likely density, such as the figure of 2·3 square metres occupied per person by a sample of North American hunters. It must be made clear however that even our present halting interpretations of this kind of evidence are more tenuous than any other conclusions we have reached so far about the way of life of prehistoric man. More and better excavation will help to clarify the situation.

These reservations made, we may look at the four most distinct types of house plan known in the late Palaeolithic. The first and simplest is round,

Right *Bone needles used to put together skin clothing, and the hole-piercer that may have been used with them.*

Below *Strings of beads, still draped about an old man buried more than 20,000 years ago, were perhaps the trimmings on long-since disintegrated clothing.*

Left *Engraving of a man, from Montastruc in the Pyrenees. He seems to have buttons up his front.*

Above *Bone, button-like discs are found at many Palaeolithic sites.*

sometimes slightly oval; its area averages about 20 square metres and it is 4 to 5 metres in diameter. There is often a hearth in the centre. A second pattern of similar size is square or slightly oblong; the known examples are paved with cobbles but have no visible hearths. A third, rather larger, oblong or three-lobed pattern classically has an area of some 40 to 50 square metres, a length of about 10 metres and three hearths in a row. The fourth and most extensive type are long houses, extending up to 30 metres or more in length. Some from Russia have nine or ten hearths in a row, grouped in threes. Their area approaches 200 square metres.

It is possible that the 20 square metre plans housed a small, or 'nuclear', family of three to six people. The 40 to 50 square metre plans may have housed the 'extended' family of ten to twenty people. The long houses could have accommodated three extended families, that is a small clan or band of thirty to sixty people.

On the basis of present information, of the four types, only the little round houses were in use before 15,000 BC. At sites like Pavlov and Dolni Vestonice in Czechoslovakia they date from about 25,000 BC. But many apparent hut sites of altogether less formalized plan are known from earlier times. Large irregularly circular habitations of about 50 square metres are known at open sites like Molodova from the end of the Mousterian, or at Arcy, under a rock shelter, from the beginning of the Upper Palaeolithic; they have hearths scattered through them. A much earlier example is the succession of oval huts at Terra Amata in Nice, which may be 200,000 years old or more. The holes left by the now rotted posts of the huts were clearly preserved here.

A round, summer tent, reconstructed from traces excavated at Borneck near Hamburg that were about 13,000 years old.

Right *Litter of mammoth bones left at the ice age hunters' camp at Dolni Vestonice.*

Below *The head of a baked clay rhinoceros from the 'artist's' hut at Dolni Vestonice.*

180

Hearths

A potentially very promising line of investigation is that of hearths, the sites of old fires represented archaeologically by burnt or blackened surfaces, or even by ash, soot and charcoal. Hallam Movius' pioneering study of the Pataud rock shelter at Les Eyzies revealed numerous hearths in the levels dating from about 21,000 BC down to the base of the Aurignacian deposits at about 32,000 BC.

At least three patterns were recognizable. At the top, a row of closely-spaced hearths of 'basin' type were found dug into the deposit along the back of the shelter and in a line. (Movius suggested a long house type of community.) In the level below was an enormous burnt area, which Movius called a bonfire hearth. (For this he inferred a large lineage kinship group.) Both could indicate larger social groups than can be inferred from the Aurignacian levels below, where the hearths were small and isolated (and the sociological interpretation is presumably of small family groups). Other Aurignacian sites in the Dordogne exhibit the same pattern, suggesting consistently smaller social units.

Pincevent

The most outstandingly successful investigation of a hut plan and a piece of pioneer research which has greatly influenced subsequent work is the excavation of Pincevent by André Leroi-Gourhan and Michel Brézillon. The site is at the confluence of the Seine and Yonne, about 60 kilometres south-east of Paris, and was probably a fording point. In 1964 it was threatened with destruction by advancing gravel works. An emergency excavation was carried out on one hut area. This was fully published in 1966; by that time a large area had been protected for scientific research and thousands of square metres have now been excavated. Pincevent dates from about 10,000 BC.

'Hut I' had three very clearly-defined hearths in a row. The outline of a three-lobed hut or tent was reconstructed from the concentration of bone and stone debris, from the extent of a covering of red ochre and from observation of the distance and direction away from a worked flint that waste flakes could be found that would fit back on to it.

This last study was most informative. A great many blades could be replaced on cores, and some small chips and spalls could be replaced on tools such as burins. By plotting lines from the cores to their component blades and flakes a series of arcs could be drawn round the hearths beyond which little debris fell. André Leroi-Gourhan took these to be the positions of the tent walls. Places where debris had obviously gone much further were thought to be openings in the walls. Finally some spaces within the hut confines were unusually clear of debris and interpreted as sleeping areas.

Left *Gravel-digging at Pincevent was halted only just in time when traces of a Palaeolithic dwelling place were first noticed there in 1964.*

Below *Scene of the excavation of Hut I at Pincevent. Crouching at the back, directing operations, are Professor Leroi-Gourhan (left) and his collaborator, Dr Brézillon.*

Distribution of red ochre at the site of Hut 1 at Pincevent.

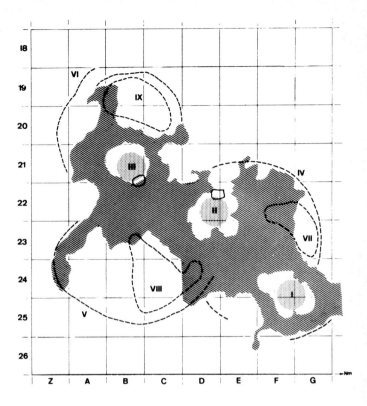

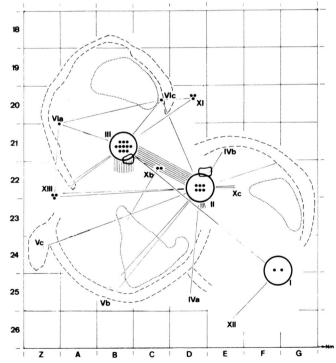

Distribution of flint cores and flakes. Dots show where cores were found; thin lines mark the paths travelled by flakes struck from them.

183

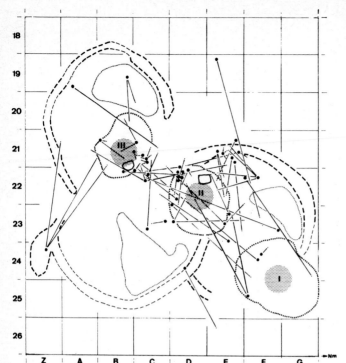

Distribution of flint burins and spalls. Large dots show where burins were found; lines mark the paths travelled by spalls (small dots) struck from them.

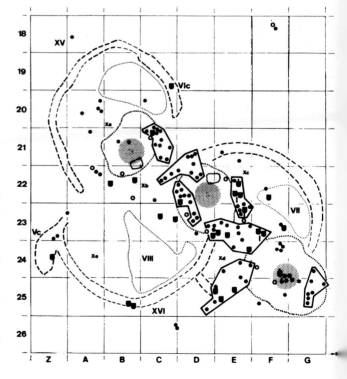

Distribution of reindeer foot bones. A concentration of whole feet, where the bones were still in anatomical connection (U-shaped symbol), was found near Hearth I. Leroi-Gourhan concluded that these had been boiled up whole for soup. Since Hearth I was sootier than Hearths II and III, and the only one with a charred reindeer foot still in it, he suggested that it had been the cooking hearth.

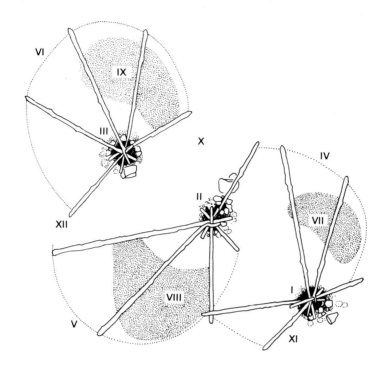

The ground plan of Hut I that became apparent as the extents and positions were plotted of all the different kinds of debris found on the floor. Leroi-Gourhan's suggested outline roughly coincides with the outer limit of the red ochre. Arcs IV, V and VI round the three lobes of the hut are drawn on the assumption that flint debris could be thrown as far as the walls and could go further only where there were entrances. Zones VII, VIII and IX were relatively free of debris and may have been sleeping areas. Hearths II and III were probably primarily intended to heat the hut. The cooking hearth (I) lay in one of the entrances, perhaps to keep smells and sooty smoke out.

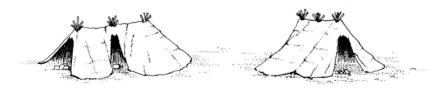

Two views of the possible above-ground appearance of Hut I.

The concentration of bones increased towards one of the hearths and the supposed opening at that end of the tent. Here alone were reindeer feet found. Leroi-Gourhan suggests that these would have been reserved for soup-making and that their presence, as well as quantities of soot, identify the cooking hearth. Large stones lying on the other two hearths would have radiated heat and are believed to have been used to warm the living area. Next to them were stone 'seats' and a great profusion of flint debris.

Chapter VIII The Rise and Fall of Cromagnon Man

The late Palaeolithic

It is widely believed that the most significant of the changes in Palaeolithic hunting society came about when the Neanderthal-Mousterian stage gave way to the Cromagnon-Upper Palaeolithic stage. Over most of the world, as far as we know, neo-sapiens, alias Cromagnon or modern type man, succeeded palaeo-sapiens, alias Neanderthal man, and other archaic hominids; the survival in neo-sapiens of some Neanderthal features suggests, however, the slow evolution of one type into another rather than the sudden appearance of a new species. Meanwhile, archaeological assemblages with blade tools predominant replace flake tool assemblages. Standardized bone tools appear, as do representational painting and engraving, personal adornment and musical instruments. But the very speed with which the changes were taking place is perhaps the most significant development; distinct new assemblages of excavated material appear in the archaeological record of this time at shorter intervals than ever before. And that this was due to accelerated local initiative rather than to the arrival of successive alien cultures is indicated in some of them by an obvious continuity of style. The name generally used for this period of innovation and rapid change is Upper Palaeolithic.

It is by no means easy to establish a precise date for the beginning of the Upper Palaeolithic or for the emergence of Cromagnon man. It may be more realistic to think of a period of some thousands of years of transition to them. Although there is no good sample of any fossil population from between 35,000 and 25,000 BC we find that a reasonably typical Cromagnon population was in existence in Czechoslovakia by 25,000 BC. No undoubted blade tool assemblages fully characteristic of the Upper Palaeolithic are reliably dated earlier than about 35,000 BC. The transition thus seems to have been made between about 40,000 and 30,000 BC. In most cases it appears to be of local origin. France's Chatelperron culture, the first in that country in which we find blade tools dominant, can be derived stylistically from a foregoing Mousterian culture in the same area. The first central European blade tool culture, the Szeletian, is equally clearly derived from a local Mousterian. The transition seems to have affected the entire area between the Atlantic, the Himalayas and the Sahara. Characteristics of the Upper Palaeolithic are widespread in Europe: in Spain, France, Germany, Italy, Czechoslovakia, Greece, the Don basin, the Crimea and the Caucasus region of Russia. In Asia, a kind of Upper Palaeolithic is found in Siberia, in the east Mediterranean (Israel and Lebanon), in Iraq and in Afghanistan. In Africa we can list Libya and Egypt. In southern Africa, however, it has been claimed that blade tools were not in use until about 10,000 BC. The situation is obscure in India and in the south-east Asian regions and in China. In Australia blade tool assemblages are believed to date only from about 4000 BC and they seem never to have reached Tasmania at all.

The late Palaeolithic appears to have seen the occupation of considerable new territory, with or without Upper Palaeolithic features. Siberia was probably the largest area added in the Old World—some time before 20,000 BC. And the far north may have been occupied for the first time in this last glacial period, for Mousterian and Upper Palaeolithic sites have been identified in the Pechora river area in northern European Russia, close to the Arctic Circle, where no earlier traces of man are found. It is from about 25,000 BC that we have good evidence of man in Australia. But most opinion on the first occupation of America favours the arrival of man across the Bering Strait from Siberia at a time when the sea level was low and the route easy, and there is still no concrete evidence of it before the closing stages of the last ice age. It may be that man was there before 12,000 BC but it has yet to be adequately demonstrated.

The climate during the late Palaeolithic in Europe seems to have remained consistently cold, with the exception of short episodes, still little understood, when a slight improvement may have set in. It was not until about 10,000 BC that the climate warmed up permanently and then very rapidly. Meanwhile animals of the tundra frequented the middle latitudes and the temperate forest was confined to more southerly latitudes than it is now.

The great age of Cromagnon man
To talk of the rise of Cromagnon man is a kind of poetic licence. His immediate predecessors, the Neanderthals, were, clearly, successful hunters, with many skills we must admire. The early Cromagnons were also successful, considerably increasing their numbers and territory, not to mention initiating the principal form of higher culture, the arts. But the last ten to fifteen thousand years of the Palaeolithic, the culminating years of Cromagnon man, were great in an even more remarkable way. We have

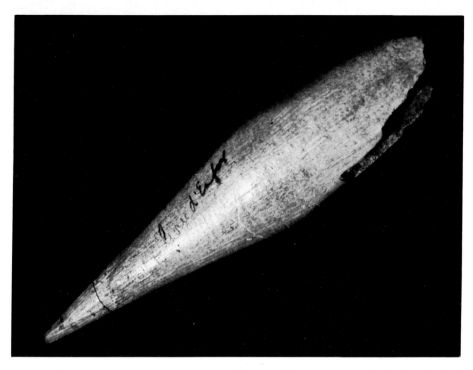

Above *With Cromagnon man appears the first use of bone for standardized tools. This split-based bone point is the earliest type known.*

Below *A broken spear thrower of about 14,000 years ago.*

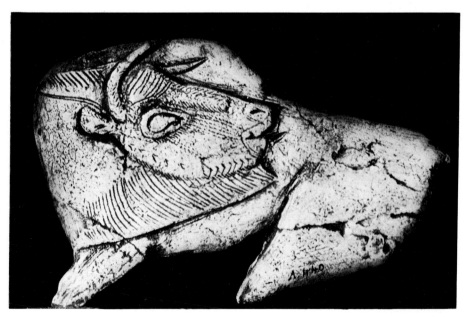

already seen how Magdalenian art marks this time out by its sheer quantity and outstanding quality. At the same time the speed of culture change was now so great that a new variety of assemblage type can be distinguished roughly every thousand years, more frequently than in the early years of the Upper Palaeolithic and much more frequently than in the Mousterian before that. And it is in this same period that sophisticated tailored clothing was first devised. But to these major advances can be added an impressive new technological expertise.

In the field of stone technology a big discovery was pressure flaking. This first appears after about 18,000 BC on leaf-shaped points in French assemblages; by the end of the ice age it was in use in many other areas. Subsequently stone arrow-heads over much of the world were made by this very delicate and precise method of flint-flaking. It leads to attractive-looking products which have at the same time strong and sharp edges.

Between 25,000 and 5,000 BC there is a slow (but over-all unmistakable) trend towards miniaturization in the manufacture of blade tools—the smaller the blades the greater the length of cutting edge obtained from a given amount of raw material. The most characteristic results are the microlith, or retouched bladelet, and its waste by-product, the microburin. These miniature blades, typically under 3 millimetres thick, 8 millimetres wide and 40 millimetres long, make an early appearance at sites like Krems in lower Austria in about 30,000 BC and are quite common at Pavlov five thousand years later. But they first became widespread from the last ten thousand years of the Palaeolithic. Post-glacial hunters over most of Eurasia and Africa have used microliths and we know that they normally set them into shafts of wood and bone for arrow tips or barbs.

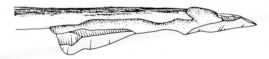

Pointed microliths were found fixed in this arrow from Løshult in Sweden. One was a tip, the other a barb.

Perhaps the most widely diffused weapon ever invented was the barbed spear or harpoon that emerged at this time. There is good evidence, in the second half of the south-west French Magdalenian, between about 14,000 and 11,000 BC, of its invention and slow elaboration; it appears in northern and eastern Europe shortly afterwards. It was later adopted by hunters in central Africa, western Asia, the Far East and Australia and its distribution extends to the southern tip of South America and to the Arctic. No other prehistoric invention achieved a wider distribution. Various fishermen of the last thousand years have used barbed harpoons and whalers used them

190

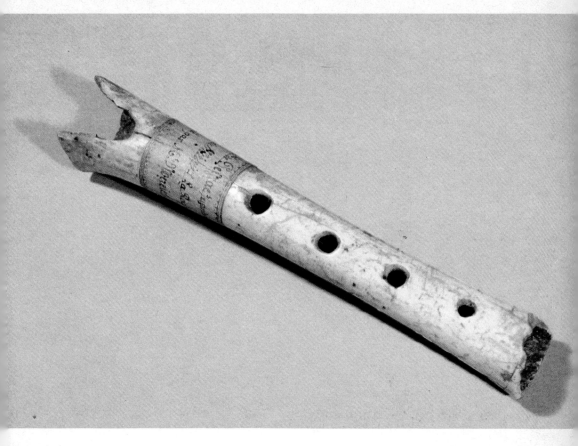

A number of hollow bones, with finger holes, come from Palaeolithic contexts. They are the earliest apparent musical instruments known.

Next page Barbed harpoons. One with only traces of barbs represents an early stage of development, another, with two rows of barbs, belongs to the culmination of the Palaeolithic. The harpoon on the left is, for comparison, a recent example from Tierra del Fuego.

191

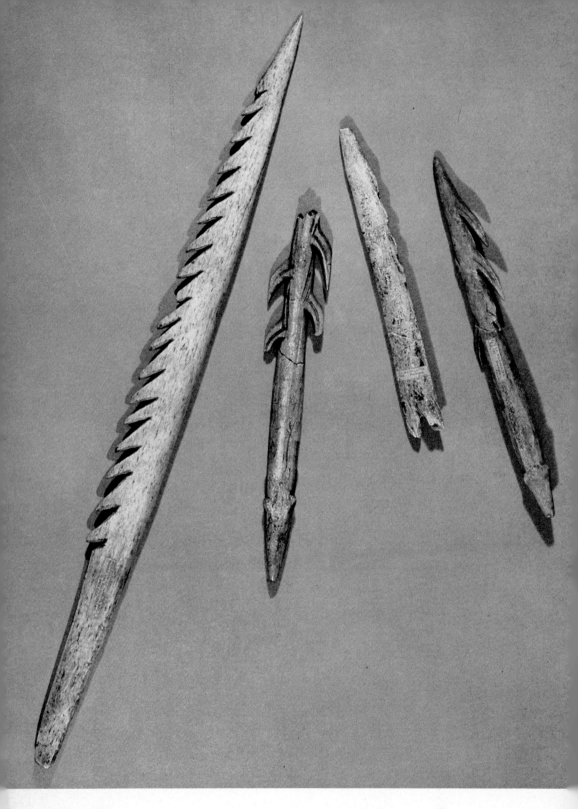

192

into the age of firearms. They are a simple device but represent a considerable improvement in hunting efficiency. An animal straining on the line attached to the head of a harpoon without barbs can easily pull off it and escape.

Functionally associated with the harpoon is the idea of propelling it with a spear thrower. This device provides the mechanical equivalent of a longer arm for the man throwing the spear. It increases both his distance and his power. Its distribution is from Australia to central America and western Europe. The earliest known comes from western Europe and dates from about 12,000 BC. It naturally tends to be used only where the bow and blow pipe are unfamiliar weapons.

But most people would accept that the premier invention of hunting society, the biggest advance in killing before firearms, was the bow. It represents a most efficient use of mechanical advantage and stored energy, and survives as a device of vital importance into medieval times. It has multiple uses, as in the bow-drill and the musical bow. Clear evidence of its early existence comes from Stellmoor near Hamburg where a settlement dated to about 8,500 BC revealed a hoard of arrows slotted for the insertion of a stone point and nocked with a bow-string groove at the other. Tanged missile points, also from the Hamburg region, probably indicate the beginning of the use of the bow from about 11,000 BC. Several earlier cultures have been credited with bows but this is on the basis of the discovery of slender missile tips which might easily be small spearheads, not arrow-heads. Bows themselves survive only from later dates than arrow-heads. The last major culture of the late Palaeolithic in France, the Magdalenian, used spear throwers but apparently not bows, being perhaps short of wood. However, of the continents inhabited by prehistoric hunters, only Australia shows no sign of having used the bow.

A bow from Holmegaard in Denmark—about 8,000 years old and the earliest bow yet discovered.

Bird darts and fish gorges seem to date from these late Palaeolithic times. In both cases carefully barbed pieces of bone or wood were probably attached to a fine line and stuffed into a morsel of bait. The date of the first fish hooks in western Europe is in some doubt, but they were used by the Natufians in the eastern Mediterranean before 8000 BC. Such inventions must have revolutionized fishing and snaring.

The first axes, which one might have expected to make a dramatic difference to man's effect on wooded environments, also appear before

8000 BC. The specimen which Semenov claims was an axe, comes from Kostenki in the Don valley and must be earlier than 12,000 BC. At British sites like Thatcham they seem to date from before 8000 BC; the fact that they appear so promptly when woods were spreading into northern Europe suggests the idea was known before. But at the moment the evidence of the impact of the axe men on the environment before the arrival of the first farmers is slight.

The earliest preserved boats, dug-out long canoes, from sites like Pesse in Holland, are post-glacial. It is however overwhelmingly likely that simple craft had already been invented in the late Palaeolithic for there are cultures of this date on either side of the western Mediterranean with strong affinities that suggest links by water transport.

This mass of innovation was made in the last ten to fifteen thousand years of the Palaeolithic and constitutes a veritable Age of Inventions— the more obvious because of its contrast with the sparsity of invention in the previous million years. This is the high point in hunting culture. I suspect it was the logical outcome, though it had taken some ten to fifteen thousand years to come to fruition, of the superior learning and problem-solving power which came with the neo-sapiens human type.

A pinewood arrow of about 10,000 years ago. It was found at Stellmoor near Hamburg. The detail shows that one end has a nock for the bowstring and the other a slot for the insertion of a flint arrow-head.

The end of the Palaeolithic

To talk of the fall of Cromagnon man is as metaphorical as it is to talk of his rise. But it has some validity in two senses. Firstly there was a dramatic change in environment as the last ice age gave way to warmer climates. For the hunters of the great reindeer herds it was an economic catastrophe. Some may have followed the herds northwards as woodlands enveloped

194

Above *As he became more adept, man fashioned smaller and smaller blades, winning a far greater length of cutting edge from a given core of flint than ever before.*

Left *A Palaeolithic lamp and other artefacts characteristic of the veritable Age of Inventions that marks the close of the Palaeolithic.*

Below *'Bird darts' were probably baited and attached to a line.*

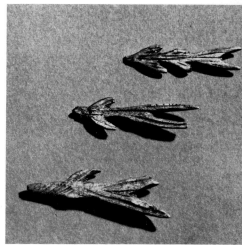

their former treeless homeland. But within a few thousand years or less we lose all track of them in the archaeological record. The high Magdalenian hunting culture, teeming with great inventions, disappears.

Another sense in which we may talk about a fall is taken from the biblical concept of the fall of man. Adam and Eve fell because they ate the forbidden fruit and were therefore subject to all the moral and social problems of modern man. Cromagnon man also ate a 'forbidden' fruit. He cultivated plants, notably wheat and barley, and within a few thousand years he was dependent on them and had passed a point of no return. His dramatically increased population could only be supported by the intensified exploitation of domestic food resources within a food-producing economy. This was helped by such factors as organized irrigation and a high degree of centralized control over the conduct of the farming. Within a few hundred years, descendants of the classless hunters found themselves peasants, tied to the land and near the base of a pyramidal hierarchy with rulers, nobles, warriors, priests and scribes standing above them. A fall indeed!

There are still great uncertainties about the precise nature and timing of the domestication of plants and animals. The first stage was almost certainly accomplished in the period between 18,000 and 8000 BC. It is claimed that wheat and probably barley were beginning to be domesticated in places like northern Iraq between 10,000 and 8000 BC. Recently there have been indications that some sort of cultivation began rather earlier in south-east Asia, though based on different crops. Rice was the key crop in some areas; maize in the New World. But in Europe and across to India and down to the Sahara the standard domesticates were sheep, goat, cattle and pigs, wheat and barley.

In the opinion of many archaeologists the development of farming was a revolutionary step though not necessarily a very difficult one on an intellectual plane. A few inventions like the sickle and quern helped. One of the most skilful advances lay in selecting suitable grains to resow. Some wild varieties would have been more suitable than others; some would have had mutations of great potential value to the farmer. A good yield would be sought, but also resistance to drought. The ears of corn which could be reaped with a sickle without 'shattering' or falling apart, would be the most convenient.

The invention of a viable system of food-production, giving unprecedented control over the food supply, takes its place as an obvious climax to the Palaeolithic Age of Inventions. Notwithstanding the exploitation and higher scale of belligerence it brought with it, the transition to farming allowed the prosperity, security and leisure which have given us science and the developed arts. Without this so called Neolithic Revolution at the close of the Palaeolithic, we simply would not be here taking an interest in our past.

Previous page *It was the domestication of plants and animals, leading to a controlled food supply and the beginning of a settled life, that brought an end to the nomadic, hunting ways of ice age man.*

Below *Footprints left by ice age man in the soft floor of Niaux cave.*

List of illustrations

LINE DRAWINGS

Page

21 Mammoth bones reconstructed as a unicorn by Otto von Guericke.

32 Time spiral. Drawing by Lovell Johns.

37 Climatic regions of Europe, Asia and Africa during maximum glaciation. Map by Lovell Johns.

38 Section through the cliffs at Weybourne, Norfolk. Drawing by Oxford Illustrators, after Clement Reid.

44 Interglacial climatic regions of Europe, Asia and Africa. Map by Lovell Johns.

61 Giant Irish deer. By courtesy of the Trustees of the British Museum (Natural History).

66 Toothrows of gorilla, *Australopithecus africanus* and modern man. Drawing by Oxford Illustrators, after Le Gros Clark.

70 Skulls of *Australopithecus africanus*, *A. robustus*, *Homo erectus* and modern man. Drawing by Oxford Illustrators, after David Pilbeam.

81 Where fossil man has been found. Map by Lovell Johns.

87 Indications of human workmanship on a flint. Drawing by Oxford Illustrators.

89 The prepared core technique of flint-flaking. Drawing by Oxford Illustrators.

99 Tip of the spear from Lehringen. Drawing by Oxford Illustrators.

139 Bone tube with artist's ochre still in it. From Grottes des Cottes. Drawing by Oxford Illustrators.

Page

157 Bison-man. From les Trois Frères. By courtesy of the late Siegfried Giedion.

179 Palaeolithic hut reconstructed from traces found at Borneck. Drawing by Oxford Illustrators, after Alfred Rust.

183 Distribution of red ochre on hut floor at Pincevent. Plan by courtesy of André Leroi-Gourhan and Michael Brézillon.

183 Distribution of flint cores and flakes on hut floor at Pincevent. Plan by courtesy of André Leroi-Gourhan and Michel Brézillon.

184 Distribution of flint burins and spalls on hut floot at Pincevent. Plan by courtesy of André Leroi-Gourhan and Michel Brézillon.

184 Distribution of animal bones on hut floor at Pincevent. Plan by courtesy of André Leroi-Gourhan and Michel Brézillon.

185 Reconstruction of the plan of the hut at Pincevent. Drawing by Oxford Illustrators, after Leroi-Gourhan.

185 Reconstruction of the above-ground appearance of the hut at Pincevent. Drawing by Oxford Illustrators, after Leroi-Gourhan.

190 Arrow, tipped with microliths. From Løshult. Drawing by Oxford Illustrators.

193 Yew bow. From Holmegaard. Drawing by Oxford Illustrators.

194 Pinewood arrow. From Stellmoor. Drawing by Oxford Illustrators.

Page

Page

6 Lascaux. Paintings in the 'shaft of the dead man'. By courtesy of the Caisse Nationale des Monuments Historiques, Paris. Photo: Jean Vertut.

11 Charles Darwin. Photo: Mansell Collection.

11 Sir Charles Lyell. From *The Illustrated London News*, 1865. Photo: Ronan Picture Library.

11 Sir John Evans. By courtesy of the Society of Antiquaries of London. Photo: John R. Freeman and Co. Ltd.

11 Handaxe found by John Evans at Amiens in 1859. By courtesy of the Department of Antiquities, Ashmolean Museum, Oxford.

14 The château at Les Eyzies. From *Reliquiae Aquitanicae*, 1875. Photo: Institute of Archaeology, London.

19 Flints found in the cave earths of the Dordogne by Lartet and Christy. From *Reliquiae Aquitanicae*, 1875. Photo: Institute of Archaeology, London.

19 Engraved bone objects found in the cave earths of the Dordogne by Lartet and Christy. From *Reliquiae Aquitanicae*, 1875. Photo: Institute of Archaeology, London.

20 The Vézère valley looking downstream from Castelmerle. Photo: Desmond Collins.

20 Cave earth from a rock shelter at Les Eyzies. By courtesy of the Department of Antiquities, Ashmolean Museum, Oxford.

24 Excavation of elephants at Aveley, 1964. By courtesy of A. J. Sutcliffe.

24 Mammoth engraved on mammoth ivory. From *Reliquiae Aquitanicae*, 1875. Photo: Institute of Archaeology, London.

25 Excavation of a mammoth at the Beresovska river, Siberia. Photo: Novosti Press Agency.

29 Solutrian flint points. From *Reliquiae Aquitanicae*, 1875. Photo: Institute of Archaeology, London.

29 Magdalenian bone harpoons. From *Reliquiae Aquitanicae*, 1875. Photo: Institute of Archaeology, London.

39 The antarctic ice cap. By courtesy of Hunting Aerosurveys Ltd.

39 Glacial striation at Val Camonica. Photo: Desmond Collins.

43 *Azolla filiculoides*.

43 Pollen grains (*Abies*, *Corylus* and *Tilia*) from Marks Tey. Photo: Charles Turner.

46 Horses painted on the cave walls at Lascaux. By courtesy of the Caisse Nationale des Monuments Historiques, Paris. Photo: Jean Vertut.

46 Fossil shells (*Theodoxus serratiliniformis*) from Swanscombe. By courtesy of Desmond Collins. Photo: Horst Kolo.

55 Russian tundra. By courtesy of the Royal Geographical Society.

55 Steppe land in Burgenland, Austria. By courtesy of the Austrian National Tourist Office.

56 Siberian reindeer herd. Photo: Novosti Press Agency.

56 Bobak marmot. By courtesy of the Zoological Society of London.

56 Arctic fox. By courtesy of the Zoological Society of London.

57 Ibex. © Bille. Photo: Natural History Photographic Agency.

60 Mammoth. Engraving, from Pech Merle. Photo: Elsevier.

60 Hippopotamus. Queen Elizabeth Park, Uganda. Photo: Hutchison Picture Library.

60 Sitatunga. By courtesy of the Zoological Society of London.

64 Chimpanzee on all fours. By courtesy of the Zoological Society of London.

64 Juvenile chimpanzee skull. Photo: Terry Dennett.

64 Modern man's skull. Photo: Professor John Napier.

67 Upper jaw of *Ramapithecus*. Photo: Imitor.

71 Adult skull of *Australopithecus africanus* from Sterkfontein. By courtesy of the Trustees of the British Museum (Natural History).

71 Skull of *Australopithecus robustus* from Swartkrans. By courtesy of the Trustees of the British Museum (Natural History). Photo: Imitor.

71 Leopard's tooth marks in a *robustus* skull

from Swartkrans. By courtesy of Dr. C. K. Brain, Transvaal Museum.

71 Skull of *Homo habilis*, hominid 24 from Olduvai. By courtesy of the late Louis Leakey. Photo: Richard E. Beatty.

77 Reconstruction by Gerassimov of Peking man (*Homo erectus* from Choukoutien). By courtesy of the late Mikhail Gerassimov.

77 Restored skull of Peking man (*Homo erectus* from Choukoutien). By courtesy of the Trustees of the British Museum (Natural History).

77 Skull of *Homo sapiens* from Steinheim. By courtesy of the Trustees of the British Museum (Natural History).

78 Skull of *Homo sapiens* from the Arago cave at Tautavel. By courtesy of Henry de Lumley.

84 Lower gorge at Olduvai. Photo: Imitor.

84 Chimpanzee 'angling' for termites. By courtesy of Mark Leighton.

84 Chopping tool. By courtesy of Desmond Collins. Photo: Horst Kolo.

88 François Bordes. Photo: Desmond Collins.

88 Stone tools made by Australian aborigines. By courtesy of the Trustees of the British Museum.

88 Levallois flakes and core. By courtesy of Stanley Thomas.

93 The wear on flint flakes after scraping bone, whittling wood, slicing meat and preparing hide. By courtesy of Lawrence Keeley.

97 Bushmen in the Kalahari. Photo: Hutchison Picture Library.

107 Making fire with a drill. Photo: Science Museum, Bryant and May Collection.

107 Making a fire by striking a spark from iron pyrites. Photo: Science Museum, Bryant and May Collection.

107 Fire plough. Photo: Science Museum, Bryant and May Collection.

108 Interior of the cave at Niaux. By courtesy of Editions Eidos, Geneva. Photo: Stevan Célébonovic.

112 Skull of Neanderthal man from Gibraltar. By courtesy of the Trustees of the British Museum (Natural History).

115 Mikhail Gerassimov. Photo: Novosti Press Agency.

115 Reconstruction by Gerassimov of the juvenile Neanderthal from le Moustier. By courtesy of the late Mikhail Gerassimov.

115 Reconstruction by Gerassimov of the Neanderthal from la Chapelle. By courtesy of the late Mikhail Gerassimov.

117 Mouth of the Shanidar cave, Iraq. Photo: Ralph S. Solecki.

123 Neanderthal skeleton (no. 4) found buried in the Shanidar cave. Photo: Ralph S. Solecki.

125 Skull of juvenile Neanderthal from Teshik Tash in the Himalayas. By courtesy of the Trustees of the British Museum (Natural History).

125 Reconstruction by Gerassimov of the juvenile Neanderthal from Teshik Tash. By courtesy of the late Mikhail Gerassimov.

131 Interior of the cave at Pech Merle. By courtesy of André Leroi-Gourhan and Editions Mazenod, Paris. Photo: Jean Vertut.

134 Bison. Modelled in clay, from Tuc d'Audoubert. The Begouen Collection. Photo: Jean Vertut. © Spadem, Paris. 1974.

134 Fish. Engraving, from Abri du Poisson. Photo: Jean Vertut.

136 Outline of hands on the wall of the cave at Pech Merle. Photo: Jean Vertut.

136 Bison. Painting, with 'shading', from Niaux. By courtesy of Editions Eidos, Geneva. Photo: Stevan Célébonovic.

136 Deer. Paint applied with the finger tips, from Covalanas. Photo: Desmond Collins.

141 Horse. Painting, with 'blocking', from Lascaux. By courtesy of the Caisse Nationale des Monuments Historiques. Photo: Jean Vertut.

141 Tectiform symbol. Painting, from Lascaux. By courtesy of the Caisse Nationale des Monuments Historiques. Photo: Jean Vertut.

144 Human figure. Painting, from Cougnac. Photo: Jean Vertut.

144 Frieze of rhinoceroses. Engraving, from Rouffignac. © M. Plassard, Grottes de Rouffignac. Photo: Jean Vertut.

145 Bison. Painted, and obscured by runs of stalactite, from Niaux. By courtesy of André Leroi-Gourhan and Editions Mazenod, Paris. Photo: Jean Vertut.

Page

148 Male figure. Engraving on bone, from Pin Hole cave. By courtesy of the Trustees of the British Museum.

148 Bison. Engraved on stone, from Bruniquel. By courtesy of the Trustees of the British Museum.

148 Carved antler baton, from the Pyrenees. By courtesy of Editions Eidos, Geneva. Photo: Stevan Célébonovic.

151 'Venus'. Modelled in clay, from Dolni Vestonice. By courtesy of the Moravske Museum, Brno. Photo: Elsevier.

152 'Venus'. From Grimaldi. By courtesy of Editions Eidos, Geneva. Photo: Stevan Célébonovic.

152 Vulvar symbols. Carved and engraved in stone, from Abri du Poisson, la Ferrassie and Pergouset. By courtesy of Desmond Collins and Editions Mazenod, Paris. Photos: Desmond Collins, Desmond Collins and Jean Vertut.

158 Human figures. Engraving, from Addaura. By courtesy of Editions Eidos, Geneva. Photo: Stevan Célébonovic.

162 Masai tribesman, Tanzania. Photo: Hutchison Picture Library.

162 Fish. Engraving, from Niaux. By courtesy of Editions Eidos, Geneva. Photo: Stevan Célébonovic.

162 Bird. Engraving, from Puy de Lacan. By courtesy of Editions Eidos, Geneva. Photo: Stevan Célébonovic.

169 *Homo sapiens*. Double burial at Sungir. Photo: Novosti Press Agency.

170 Horse. Carving, from Sungir. Photo: Novosti Press Agency.

170 Head. Carved in ivory, from Brassempouy. By courtesy of Editions Eidos, Geneva. Photo: Stevan Célébonovic.

175 'Necklace' of perforated teeth, beads and shells from Bruniquel and other Dordogne sites and from Mentone. By courtesy of the Trustees of the British Museum. Photo: Horst Kolo.

175 Glutton. Carved on bone pendant, from the Dordogne. By courtesy of the Trustees of the British Museum.

Page

177 Two bone needles from Bruniquel and a flint piercer from Laugerie Haute. By courtesy of the Trustees of the British Museum. Photo: Horst Kolo.

177 *Homo sapiens*. Burial at Sungir. Photo: Novosti Press Agency.

178 Human figure, with 'buttons'. Engraving on bone, from Montastruc. By courtesy of André Leroi-Gourhan and Editions Mazenod, Paris. Photo: Jean Vertut.

178 Button-like disc. From Laugerie Basse. By courtesy of the Musée du Périgord, Périgueux. Photo: Elsevier.

180 Mammoth bones at Dolni Vestonice. Photo: Desmond Collins.

180 Head of a rhinoceros. Modelled in clay, from Dolni Vestonice. By courtesy of the Moravske Museum, Brno. Photo: Jean Vertut.

182 Gravel-digging in 1964 at the site of excavations at Pincevent. By courtesy of André Leroi-Gourhan.

182 Excavations at Pincevent. By courtesy of André Leroi-Gourhan.

189 Split-based bone point, from Gorge d'Enfer. By courtesy of the Trustees of the British Museum. Photo: Horst Kolo.

189 Part of a spear thrower in the form of a bison, carved in antler, from la Madeleine. By courtesy of the Musée des Antiquités Nationales, Saint Germain. Photo: Jean Vertut.

195 Microliths. Flint, from Bruniquel. By courtesy of the Trustees of the British Museum. Photo: Horst Kolo.

195 Lamp, burins and a perforated pebble. From Magdalenian sites. By courtesy of Editions Eidos, Geneva. Photo: Stevan Célébonovic.

195 Bird darts. Bone, from Bruniquel. By courtesy of the Trustees of the British Museum. Photo: Horst Kolo.

197 Ripening wheat. Photo: Robert Harding Associates.

198 Footprints of ice age man in the cave at Niaux. By courtesy of Editions Eidos, Geneva. Photo: Stevan Célébonovic.

COLOUR PHOTOGRAPHS

Page

17 Handaxe found at Hoxne in 1797 by John Frere. By courtesy of the Society of Antiquaries of London. Photo: John R. Freeman & Co. Ltd.

18 Red deer. Painting, from Lascaux. By courtesy of Editions Mazenod, Paris. Photo: Jean Vertut.

35 Skull of juvenile *Australopithecus africanus*. From Taung. Photo: Imitor.

36 Savannah. Photo: Alan Hutchison Picture Library.

101 Mammoth. Carved bone, from Bruniquel. By courtesy of the Trustees of the British Museum.

102 Mammoth. Engraving, from Arcy. Photo: Jean Vertut.

119 Neanderthal skull cap. From the Feldhof cave, Neanderthal. Photo: Imitor.

120 Levallois blade and flake. By courtesy of Desmond Collins. Photo: Horst Kolo.

Page

137 Bison. Painting, from Font de Gaume. By courtesy of André Leroi-Gourhan. Photo: Jean Vertut.

138 Bison and horse. Engraving, from Gabillou. Photo: Jean Vertut.

155 Perforated baton. Engraved antler, from la Madeleine. By courtesy of the Trustees of the British Museum. Photo: Horst Kolo.

156 Engraved antler, from Bruniquel. By courtesy of the Trustees of the British Museum.

173 The Volgu blade: a leaf-shaped Solutrian point. By courtesy of the Trustees of the British Museum. Photo: Horst Kolo.

174 Hearths in the Palaeolithic hut floor at Pincevent. By courtesy of André Leroi-Gourhan. Photo: Jean Vertut.

191 Bone flute. From the Vézère valley. By courtesy of the Trustees of the British Museum. Photo: Horst Kolo.

192 Barbed harpoons from la Madeleine and a latter-day specimen from Tierra del Fuego. By courtesy of the Trustees of the British Museum. Photo: Horst Kolo.

Index

Page numbers in italic refer to illustrations and their captions

Abbeville, 12–13
Aborigines, 114; stone tools, 91; *88*
Abri du Poisson, 133; *152*
Acheulian: culture tradition, 100; assemblages, 103; at Orgnac, 165
Acromegaly, 126, 128
Adams, Leith, 21, 22
Addaura, *158*
Afghanistan, 188
Africa: barbed spears, 190; Cromagnon man, 188; environment during ice ages, 62; evolution of hominids in, 70–5; *Homo erectus* in, 76–9, 98; prehistoric art, 135; prehistoric population, 161–3; stone tools, 85–6, 92–3
Agassiz, Jean Louis, 34
Agriculture, advent of, 196
Algeria, 76
Alpera, 172
Altamira, 132, 135, 139, 142
Ambrona, 92
America, ice ages, 31, 34, 40
Andalucia, 132
Angles-sur-l'Anglin, 132, 133
Animals: in cave art, 139–40, 147, 149; and dating techniques, 45–6; during ice ages, 59–61
Apes: brain size, 128; and the evolution of man, 63–5; similarities between juvenile apes and modern man, 127
L'Arago, 80; *77*
Arcy sur Cure, 132, 135, 179; *102*
Arrow-heads, 190; *190*
Arrows, *194*
Asia: barbed spears, 190; Cromagnon man, 188; environment during ice ages, 62; *Homo erectus*, 98
Aurignacian period: cave art, 150–3, 157; hearths, 181
Australia: aboriginal stone tools, 91; *88*; aborigines, 114; barbed spears, 190; cremations, 168; Cromagnon man, 188; fire-making, 106; primitive art, 135, 139; remains of early man in, 76
Australopithecus, 66, 68
Australopithecus africanus, 70–5, 82, 95, 96, 127, 161; *33, 35, 70, 71, 81*
Australopithecus robustus, 70, 72–3, 74, 95, 96, 127, 161; *70, 71, 81*
Axes, 193–4

Baboons: infant mortality, 160; population density, 163
Bader, Otto, 171
Baikal, lake, 172
Baringo, 75
Barma Grande, 168
'Baton de commandement', *155*
Beads: on clothing, 171–2; *177*; in head-dresses, 168; necklaces, 171; *175*
Beer, Sir Gavin de, 126
Belcayre, 135
Belleforest, François de, 143
Bergmann, 100
Bilzingsleben, 80
'Bird darts', 193; *195*
Blanchard rock shelter, 153
Boats, 194
Bone: bone tools, 28, 83–5; *29, 189*; cave deposits, 109; and dating techniques, 49, 53–4
Bordes, François, 54, 92; *88*
Borneck, *179*
Boule, Marcellin, 66, 68, 111–13, 114–16, 118
Bourgeois, abbé, 86
Bouyssonie, A. and J., 111
Bows, 193; *193*
Brace, C. Loring, 111, 124
Brain, size of: *Australopithecus*, 66; *Australopithecus africanus*, 72, 74; *Australopithecus robustus*, 73; and childbirth, 128; chimpanzee, 65, 68, 72; gorillas, 65; *Homo erectus*, 76, 79; *Homo habilis*, 74; Java man, 66, 75; modern man, 65; Neanderthal man, 127–8; Peking man, 76, 79; *Ramapithecus*, 68; Solo man, 76; Steinheim skull, 79; Swanscombe skull, 79
Brassempouy, *170*

Breton, André, 143
Breuil, abbé, 86, 116, 140, 142, 143, 146
Brézillon, Michel, 181; *182*
Bristlecone pine, 50, 51–2
British Association for the Advancement of Science, 12, 113
Brno, 121
Broken Hill, 79
Brose, 122
Bruniquel, 156; *101, 148*
Buckland, Dean William, 9, 12
Buret, 172
Burials, 166–8; *169, 170*
Bushmen, 128, 153, 176; *97, 152*

Campbell, Bernard, 80
Cantabria, cave paintings, 130, 132
Cap Blanc, 133
Cartailhac, Emile, 142
Carvings, 16, 27, 94, 129, 133–5, 150–4, 157–9; *24, 101, 102, 134, 138, 148, 151, 152, 155, 156, 158, 162, 175, 178*
Castanet rock shelter, 150
Cave, A. J., 114–16
Cave-dwelling, 103–5, 106, 109–10; *108*
Cave paintings, 16, 27, 45, 129, 130–3, 135–59, 172; *18, 46, 131, 136, 137, 141, 144*
La Chaise, 80
Chancelade man, 122
La Chapelle-aux-Saints, 113–14, 116, 121, 122, 128, 167; *115*
Chatelperron culture, 187–8
Childbirth, and brain size, 128
Childe, V. Gordon, 28–30
Chimpanzees, *64*; brain size, 65, 68, 72; climatic adaptation, 100; and evolution of man, 63–5; teeth, *64*; tool-using, 83; *84*
China: *Homo erectus*, 76, 100; Neanderthal remains in, 122
Chopping tools, 90, 92
Choukoutien, 76, 100, 104, 165; *77*
Christy, Henry, 15–16, 23, 27, 90, 103, 109, 110, 130, 142, 147
Chronometric dating, 48–54
Circeo, skull from, 128
Clacton, 99
Clactonian: culture tradition, 100; assemblages, 103
Clark, Desmond, 94
Clay-modelling, 133; *134, 180*
Climate: Cromagnon man's adaptation to, 194; Neanderthal man's adaptation to, 122–4, 126; Palaeolithic, 171, 188; *see also* Ice ages
Clothing and adornment, Cromagnon man, 168–72
Cogul, 172
Les Combarelles, 27, 130
Combe Grenal, 47, 109
Commarque, 133
Coon, Carleton, 76, 79, 124
Les Cottes, 135
Cougnac, 142, 146, 154, 157; *144*
Cova Negra, 80
Covalanas, 139; *136*
Crelin, Edmund, 116
Cremations, 168
Crimea, 126
Cromagnon man, 187–96; *33*; cave painting, 8,

113; climatic adaptation, 122; clothing and adornment, 168–72; distribution, *81*; evolution from Neanderthal man, 118–21, 124; life expectancy, 160; organized burials, 167, 168; skulls, 80, 126; tool-making, 190–4
Cromer, geological deposits, 38; *38*
Cuvier, Baron Georges, 9, 22
Czechoslovakia: burials, 168; Cromagnon man, 187, 188; huts, 179; Neanderthal man, 121; stone tools, 94

Danube tributaries, river terraces of, 47
Darwin, Charles, 8, 10–12, 26–7, 66, 68; *11*
Dating techniques, 27–8; chronometric dating, 48–54; loess deposits, 47; and mammals, 45–7; Palaeolithic art, 150–4; pollen analysis, 40–5, 109; *43*; Potassium-Argon dating, 31, 52–3; radiocarbon dating, 8, 31, 41, 49, 50–2, 109; river terraces, 47–8; silt layers, 49–50; tree rings, 49, 50, 51–2; uranium, 53–4, 109
Deevey, Edward, 161–3
Dendrochronology, 50
Denmark, bow from, *193*
Derbyshire, 104; *148*
Diet, 164–5; meat-eating, 95–6
Diffusionism, 27, 28
Dobzhansky, T., 126
Dolni Vestonice, 150, 179; *151, 180*
Don valley, 188, 194
Dordogne: cave art, 129, 132, 153, 154; *175*; cave sediments, 109; early excavations, 13–21; Neanderthal settlements, 104; Neanderthal skulls, 126; possible tundra conditions in, 54–8
Dos Aguas, 172
Douar Doum, 85
Dryopithecus, 15
Dubois, Eugène, 75

East Rudolf, 74, 76–9, 86
Egypt, Cromagnon man, 188
Ehringsdorf, 166
Elephas antiquus, 22, 61, 79; *24*
Elephas primigenius, 21
Elliot Smith, Sir Grafton, 27, 30, 66, 111, 116
Engravings, *see* Carvings
Eocene, 34
Eolithic, 86–7
'Eoliths', 86–7
Escoural, 132
Eskimos, 122
Etcheberriko-Karbia, 132
Ethiopia: hominid remains, 74, 75; possible habitation structures, 98
Europe: *Homo erectus*, 98; ice ages, 31, 34, 40
Evans, Sir John, 13, 90; *11*
Evolution, theory of, 10–12, 26–30
Evolutionism, 27, 28
Les Eyzies, 13–16, 130, 133, 143, 181, *14, 20, 134*

Falconer, Hugh, 13, 16, 22
Feldhof, *119*
Ferguson, Charles Wesley, 50
La Ferrassie, 121, 128, 129, 135, 150, 153, 160, 167; *152*
Fire-making, 100, 105–6; *107*
Flaking, stone tools, 87–90, 94, 174, 190; *87, 120*
Fluorine, in dating techniques, 49
Font de Gaume, 27, 130, 135, 139; *137*

Fontéchevade, 80, 118, 122
Food: diet, 95–6, 164–5; preparation, 106, 124
Forbes, 38, 40
Fossils: early interpretations of, 9; as source material in cave research, 109
Fourneau du Diable, 133, 154
France: bone needles, 171; cave art, 94, 130–9, 142–7, 153–7; cave-dwelling, 104; Chatelperron culture, 187–8; Cromagnon man, 188; early excavations, 13–21; pre-Neanderthal remains, 80; loess deposits, 47; musical instruments, 176; Neanderthal remains, 113–14; stone tools, 86, 91, 94
Frere, John, 8–9, 41

Gabillou, 159; *138*
Gardar skull, 126
Geer, Baron de, 49–50
Geology, early theories of, 9–10
Gerassimov, Mikhail, *115*
Gibraltar skull, 113, 122; *112*
Giedion, Siegfried, 140–2, 149–50, 159
Gorillas, teeth, *66*
Gould, Richard, 91
Gouy, 130
Gower peninsula, 104
Grave goods, 167
Greece, 188
Greenland, 126
Grimaldi caves, 118, 168; *152*
'Grimaldi negroids', 118
Guericke, Otto von, 21

Hadar basin, 75
Hadza tribe, 165
Hamburg, 193
Handaxes, 9, 85, 90, 91, 92, 94, 98, 100, 104; *11, 17, 88*
Harrison, Benjamin, 86
Hauser, Otto, 113–14
Head-dresses, Cromagnon man, 168–71, 172; *170*
Hearths, 181, 186; *174, 183, 184, 185*
Hockett, Charles, 96
Holmegaard, bow from, *193*
Hominids, evolution of, 68–75
Homo erectus, 70–9, 82, 98–100, 127, 171; *33, 70, 77, 81*
'*Homo gardarensis*', 126
Homo habilis, 74, 99; *71, 81*
Homo neanderthalensis, see Neanderthal man
Homo sapiens, 54, 63, 70, 72, 73, 75, 76, 79–82, 122, 127; *33, 70, 77, 78, 81, 169, 170*
Horses, evolution of, 45; *46*
Howell, Clark, 122
Hoxne, 9, 23, 26, 41–2; handaxe from, *17*
Human figures, in cave art, 157–9; *144, 148, 151, 152, 157, 158, 170, 178*
Hungary, *Homo erectus*, 100
Hunting: development of, 95–6, 99; rituals, 166; techniques, 165–6
Hunting societies, 163–5
Huts, 98, 176–86; *174, 182, 183, 184, 185*
Hutton, James, 9–10, 23, 90–1
Huxley, Thomas Henry, 26–7, 66, 113
Hypermorphy, 82, 126, 127

Ice ages, 31–62; Alpine glaciations, 47; *33, 37*
India, Cromagnon man, 188

Infant mortality, 160, 161
Ipswich, 42
Iran, Neanderthal remains, 122
Iraq: advent of agriculture, 196; Cromagnon man, 188; Neanderthal remains, 122
Isaac Glynn, 98
Isimila, 92
Israel, 188; Neanderthal skeletons, 121
Isturitz, 153, 154, 171, 172
Italy, 188; cave art, 132

Java man, 27, 66, 70, 75–6, 113, 126
Jerusalem, 104

Kalahari Bushmen, *97*
Kanam, 86, 118
Kanjera skull, 118
Kapovo, 132
Keeley, Lawrence, 92
Keith, Sir Arthur, 126
Kent's Cavern, 12, 104
Kenya, hominid remains, 74
King, William, 113
Kostenki, 194
Krems, 190
Kromdraai, 72

Labattut, 150
Laetolil, 75
Lalinde, 157, 159
Lamarck, 63
Language, Neanderthal man, 96, 116
Lantien, 76
Lartet, Edouard, 15–21, 26, 27, 109, 110, 130, 142, 147
Lascaux, 8, 13, 45, 130, 139, 142–3, 154; *18, 46, 141*
Laugerie Basse, 16, 154
Laugerie Haute, 109
Laussel, 133, 172
Lazaret, 80
Leakey, Louis, 70, 85, 118
Lebanon, Cromagnon man, 188
Le Gros Clark, Sir Wilfred, 66
Lehringen, 166; *99*
Leroi-Gourhan, André, 132, 140, 154, 181, 186; *182*
Levallois flakes, 89, 90; *88, 89, 120*
Libby, Willard F., 8, 52
Libya, 188
Lieberman, Philip, 116
Life expectancy, 160–1
Lightfoot, Bishop, 8
Limeuil, 154
Loess deposits, in dating techniques, 47
Løshult, arrow from, *190*
Lothagam, 75
Lubbock, John, 23
Luquet, 147
Lyell, Sir Charles, 9–10, 26, 34–8, 40, 45; *11*

La Madeleine, 16, 23, 154, 171, 172; *24*
Magdalenian period, 28; barbed spears, 190; *29*; burials, 168; cave art, 133, 154–9; musical instruments, 176; spear-throwers, 193
Magnetism, recorded in volcanic rocks, 53
Makapan Limeworks, 72, 85, 86, 95, 96
Malta (Siberia), 171, 172

Malthus, Thomas, 12, 100
Mammoths, 16, 21–3, 45, 59–61; *21, 24, 25, 60, 101, 102, 180*
Mapa, 80
Marks Tey, 50
Mas d'Azil, 154
Masai tribe, *162*
Mauer, 76
Meiendorf, 166
Melka Kontoure, 98
Mendel, Gregor, 12
Mesolithic, 160
Microliths, 190; *190, 195*
'Missing link', 68–9
Modjokerto, 126
Moir, James Reid, 86
Molodova, 176, 179
Monogamy, 96–8, 164
Montastruc, 172; *178*
Monte Castillo, 132
Montespan, 130, 132, 147, 166
Montmaurin, 80
Moravia, 104, 121
Morocco, 85
Mortillet, Gabriel de, 27–8, 30, 85, 86, 103, 116
Mount Carmel, 121, 166
Mousterian culture, 28, 188; grave goods, 167
Le Moustier, 23, 113, 114, 122; *115*
Movius, Hallam, 54, 181
Mungo, lake, 168
Munster (Germany), 50
Musical instruments, 176; *191*
Mwanganda, 94

Natufian culture, 193
Natural selection, 10–12, 100
Neander, J., 113
Neanderthal man, 31, 79; *33, 112, 115, 119, 125*; as ancestor of *Homo sapiens*, 118, 121, 124–9, 187; brain size, 127–8; burials, 166–7, 168; *123*; climatic adaptation, 122–4, 126; distribution, *81*; early theories of, 66, 68, 111–16; extinction of, 116–22; language, 96, 116; life expectancy, 160; skulls, 80; teeth, 124
Needles, bone and flint, 171; *177*
Neoteny, 82, 126–9, 160
New Caledonia, aborigines, 114
New Guinea, primitive art, 139
Ngandong, 75
Niaux, 130, 132, 146; *108, 136, 144, 198*
Nilsson, Sven, 23
Noaillan culture, 150, 153
Nougier, L., 143, 146

Oakley, Kenneth, 48, 105, 118
Obsidian, in dating techniques, 49
Olduvai Gorge, 62, 73–4, 76, 85–6, 92, 98, 99, 166; *71, 84*
Olorgesailie, 94
Omo valley, 74, 79, 80, 85
Orgnac, 165

Paglicci, 132
Pair-non-Pair, 27
Paranthropus robustus, 72
Pataud, 121, 181
Pavlov, 179, 190
Pech de l'Azé, 126, 135

Pech Merle, 132, 139, 142, 143, 154, 157; *131, 136*
Pechora, river, 188
Peking man, 70, 76, 79, 165; *77*
Penck, Albrecht, 47
Pengelly, William, 12
Pergouset, 132; *152*
Périgord, 130, 132
Perthes, Jaques Boucher de, 12–13, 118
Pesse, 194
Petersfels, 157
Petralona, 80
Peyrony, Denis, 28
Piette, 147
Pigments, in cave paintings, 135
Piltdown man, 68, 118
Pin Hole cave, 165; *148*
Pincevent, 181–6; *174, 182, 183, 184, 185*
Pithecanthropus erectus, 75
Le Placard, 176
Pleistocene, 34–40, 47
Pliocene, 34
Pliopithecus, 15
Pollen analysis, 40–5, 109; *43*
Polygamy, 164
Population size, Palaeolithic, 161–3
Post, Lennart Von, 40
Potassium-Argon dating technique, 31, 52–3
Predmost, 121, 168, 171
Prehistoric Society of East Anglia, 86
Pressure flaking, stone tools, 190
Prestwich, Joseph, 13
Pyrenees, cave art, 130, 132, 154, 172; *148, 178*

Quercy, 132
La Quina, 91, 128

Radiocarbon dating, 8, 31, 41, 49, 50–2, 109
Raglan, Lord, 30
Ramapithecus, 68, 75; *33, 67*
Read, Catherine and Dwight, 95
Reindeer, 26, 54, 58, 59, 61, 194; *56–7*
Rhône valley, 132
Ribadesella, 132
River terraces, and dating techniques, 47–8
Robert, R., 143, 146
Robinson, John, 72, 73, 95
Le Roc de Sers, 94, 133, 154
Roermond, 166
Rouffignac, 132, 143–7; *144*
Rubidium Strontium dating technique, 52
Rudolf, lake, 74
Russia: Aurignacian statuettes, 153; Cromagnon man, 171, 188; huts, 179; musical instruments, 176; Neanderthal settlements, 104

Sahara, 163; rock art, 135
St. Acheul, 103
Saldanha, 79
Sauramo, Matti, 49
Sautuola, Don Marcelino de, 142
Schaafhausen, Professor, 113
Sculpture, *see* Carvings
Semenov, Sergei, 92, 194
Sequoia trees, 50, 51
Shanidar, 122, 127; *117, 123*
Siberia, 163; Cromagnon man, 188; statuettes, 172; stone tools, 91

Sicily, cave art, 132, 135; *158*
Silt layers, and dating techniques, 49–50
Skhul, 121
Smith, J. Maynard, 126
Sollas, William, 91, 116
Solo, river, 75–6, 80
Solutrian period, 28; bone needles, 171; cave art, 133, 154; stone tools, *29*
South America, barbed spears, 190
Spain: cave art, 130, 132, 135, 142; Cromagnon man, 188; stone tools, 92
'Spanish Levant Art', 132, 139, 172
Spears, 99, 166; *99*; barbed, 190–3; *29, 192*; spear-throwers, 193; *101, 189*
Speech, 96; Neanderthal man, 116
Spy, 116, 128
Staroselje, 126
Steatopygia, 153; *152*
Steinheim skull, 79–80, 127; *77*
Stellmoor, 193; *194*
Steppe, 58, 59; *55, 56*
Sterkfontein, 72, 86, 95, 104; *71*
Straus, William, 114–16
Sungir, 168, 171–2; *169, 170, 177*
Swanscombe, 62, 103, 166
Swanscombe skull, 79–80, 82, 118, 122, 127
Swartkrans, 72–3, 86
Sweden, arrowhead, *190*
Symbolism, cave art, 139, 140–2, 153; *141, 152*
Szeletian culture, 150, 188

Tabun, 121
Tanzania, hominid remains, 73–4, 75
Tardiguet, 85
Tata, 129
Taubach, 165
Taung, 72, 126; *35*
Tautavel, 80; *78*
Teeth: apes and monkeys, 65; *66*; *Australopithecus africanus*, 66, 72, 73, 95, 96, 161; *66*; *Australopithecus robustus*, 73, 161; chimpanzee, *64*; gorilla, *66*; *Homo habilis*, 74; modern man, 65; *66*; Neanderthal man, 124; *Ramapithecus*, *67*
Tents, *179*
Ternfine, 76
Terra Amata, 165, 179
Teshik Tash, *125*
Teyjat, 154
Thames, river terraces, 47–8
Thatcham, 194
Tierra del Fuego, harpoon from, *192*
Tito Bustillo, 132
Tool-making, 83–90
Tools, bone, 28, 83–5; *29, 189*
Tools, stone, 9, 12–13, 15–16, 116–18, 190; *11, 17, 19, 29, 84, 120, 173, 195*; flaking, 87–90,

94, 174, 190; *87, 88, 120*; uses, 90–6; *93*; *see also* Weapons
Torralba, 92, 99, 100
Tree rings, dating techniques, 49, 50, 51–2
Trinil, 75, 76
Les Trois Frères, 130, 159, 166, 176
Tuc d'Audoubert, 130, 133–5; *134*
Tundra, 54–9; *55–7*
Tylor, Edward, 15, 23

Uganda, stone tools, 85
Urals, cave art, 132
Uranium, in dating techniques, 53–4, 109

Val Camonica, 135
Vallois, H. V., 160
Vallonnet, 104
Varves, and dating techniques, 49–50
Vegetation: during ice ages, 40–5, 62; *37, 43, 44*; pollen analysis, 40–5, 109; *43*; tree ring dating, 49, 50, 51–2; tundra, 59
Verneuil, M. de, 16
Vertesszöllös, 76, 100
Vertut, Jean, 147
Vézère valley, 13, 130; *20*
Virchow, Rudolf, 113
Vogelherd, 153
Volcanic rock, as record of the earth's magnetism, 53
Volgu blade, *173*

Wales, cave-dwelling, 104
Wallace, 12
Warren, S. H., 28
Washburn, Sherwood, 66
Weapons, 99, 166, 190–4; *99, 192, 193, 194, 195*; *see also* Tools
Weiner, Joseph, 80
West, Richard, 41, 42
Westbury-sub-Mendip, 103–4
White Mountains, California, 50
Willendorf, 153
Witsen, Nicolaus, 21–2
Wolpoff, 122
Wooldridge, S. W., 47–8

Yenisei, river, 166
Yiewsley, 103
Yiwara tribe, 91
Young, J. Z., 126
Yugoslavia, 104

Zagwijn, Waldo, 42
Zambia, 79
Zlaty Kun, 121